FROM PITCH TO GLORY LEGENDS RISE

From Pitch to Glory
Legends Rise

MACK RAFEAL

UNIEK ENTERPRISES

CONTENTS

Chapter 9

152

INDEX

Chapter 8: The Peak of Glory

8.1 Culmination of Career

1. Pinnacle moments and championships
2. International recognition and awards

8.2 Passing the Torch

1. Mentoring the next generation
2. Shaping the future of the sport

Chapter 9: Conclusion

9.1 Reflection on the Journey

9.2 Looking back on a legendary career

9.3 The enduring impact on football culture

CHAPTER 1

Introduction

The idea of an acquaintance fills in as the passage with any talk, be it an insightful paper, an enthralling novel, or a convincing exposition. It is the underlying experience between the writer and the peruser, a pivotal point where the establishment for the resulting story or contention is laid. The specialty of creating an acquaintance lies in its capacity with dazzle the peruser's consideration, convey the focal proposition, and give a guide to the excursion ahead.

At its center, a presentation is a scholarly handshake, a virtual motion that lays out an association between the creator and the crowd. It establishes the vibe for the whole piece, molding the peruser's assumptions and impacting their impression of what is to come. A very much created acquaintance is associated with a greeting, enticing the peruser to dive further into the story or contention that unfurls past the underlying passages.

One of the key motivations behind an acquaintance is with frame the extension and reason for the work. Whether it is a scholastic paper looking to add to a specific field of study or a piece of exploratory writing intending to engage and incite thought, the presentation fills in as a compass, directing the peruser through the writer's goals. This navigational capability is essential in situating the crowd, furnishing them with an ability to know east from west and reason as they set out on the scholarly excursion introduced before them.

Notwithstanding direction, a powerful presentation should likewise catch the peruser's advantage. The huge ocean of data and diversion accessible in the advanced age requests that creators utilize procedures to stand apart in the midst of the clamor. This requires an imaginative and connecting with way to deal with the basic segment, one that sparkles interest and tempts the peruser to put their time and consideration in the material within reach. This could include introducing an interesting inquiry, sharing a captivating story, or divulging a frightening measurement that provokes the peruser's interest.

Besides, an acquaintance goes about as an entryway with the creator's point of view, offering a brief look into their scholarly and inventive position. This is where the writer lays out their ethos, motioning toward the peruser why they are able to examine the picked subject or portray a specific story. Whether through scholarly qualifications, individual encounters, or a mix of both, the presentation is the space for the creator to declare their believability and lay out a compatibility with the crowd.

The sequential unfurling of thoughts inside a presentation is a fragile dance, requiring the creator to offset quickness with instruction. While it ought to give sufficient setting to permit the peruser to get a handle on the overall subject, it ought to likewise shun overpowering the crowd with exorbitant subtleties. The presentation capabilities as a secret, offering a brief look at the primary story or contention without uncovering every one of its complexities. This fragile equilibrium keeps up with the peruser's advantage and urge them to continue further into the work.

In the scholastic domain, a presentation frequently finishes up with a reasonable and compact postulation explanation. This assertion fills in as the North Star, directing the peruser through the approaching investigation of thoughts. It typifies the essential contention or motivation behind the work, offering a guide for what lies ahead. Making a strong proposition proclamation requires accuracy and lucidity, as it turns into the point of convergence around which the whole piece rotates.

Past its underlying and utilitarian perspectives, a presentation is a vehicle for setting the temperament and laying out the air of the work. For example, a story presentation might utilize clear symbolism and reminiscent language to move the peruser into a particular overall setting. Interestingly, an influential presentation could use logical gadgets and convincing language to summon a need to keep moving or significance. No matter what the class or reason, the presentation fills in as the scholarly suggestion, setting up the peruser for the ensemble of thoughts that follows.

As the scholarly scene keeps on developing, so too do the assumptions put upon presentations. In the computerized age, where abilities to focus are transitory and interruptions proliferate, the test of catching and keeping up with the peruser's advantage is more articulated than any time in recent memory.

This reality highlights the significance of advancement and versatility in making presentations that resound with contemporary crowds. Writers should be sensitive to the powerful idea of peruser inclinations and utilize systems that meet as well as surpass these assumptions.

All in all, the presentation is a diverse scholarly gadget that assumes a critical part in forming the peruser's insight. It fills in as a passage, a navigational device, and a mystery for the scholarly or imaginative excursion that unfurls inside the resulting pages. The specialty of making a compelling presentation lies in finding some kind of harmony among lucidity and interest, quickness and usefulness. As the scholarly scene develops, so too should the methodologies utilized in presentations, guaranteeing they stay important and convincing in a time described by data overflow and transient abilities to focus.

1.1 Setting the Stage

Setting the Stage:

Setting the stage is a basic preface to any intelligent or inventive undertaking, a preliminary demonstration that lays out the specific circumstance, approaches the story, and presents the central participants. Similarly as a very much planned stage upgrades the exhibition of a play, a proficient setting of the stage in writing, scholastic composition, or any type of talk is instrumental in molding the peruser's comprehension and assumptions. This stage isn't just a custom however an essential move by the creator to drench the crowd on the planet they are going to investigate, establishing the groundwork for a rich and significant commitment.

In writing, setting the stage includes something beyond depicting the actual environmental elements. It envelops the worldly, social, and social milieu in which the account unfurls. The setting fills in as a scenery against what characters develop, clashes emerge, and subjects resound. For instance, a story set in Victorian Britain summons pictures of gas-lit roads, corseted figures, and unbending social orders, promptly moving the peruser into a particular verifiable and social setting. Then again, a story set in a tragic future welcomes the peruser to imagine a world portrayed by mechanical progressions, cultural rot, and a feeling of premonition.

Also, the setting isn't bound to the actual domain; it reaches out to the profound and mental scene too. The tone and air made by the creator through the setting can bring out a scope of feelings — from sentimentality and warmth to pressure and disquiet.

Consider a scene set in a sun-doused glade, where the fragrance of wildflowers blends with the delicate murmur of honey bees. Such a setting inspires sensations of quietness and tranquility, forming the peruser's personal reaction to the unfurling occasions. On the other hand, a dull and blustery night in a forsaken scene might bring out a feeling of premonition, flagging that the story is going to take a more unpropitious turn.

In the domain of scholarly composition, setting the stage includes giving the fundamental setting to the review or contention within reach. This setting fills in as the framework whereupon the ensuing examination or investigation is constructed. In logical examination, for example, setting the stage includes exploring important writing, introducing the exploration question, and framing the hole in information that the review means to address. In this specific situation, the stage-setting is a fastidious cycle that includes blending existing information, distinguishing holes or discussions, and supporting the meaning of the examination.

The stage-setting in scholastic composing isn't restricted to the presentation; it stretches out all through the work, directing the peruser through the sensible movement of thoughts. Each part, whether it be a writing survey, technique, or conversation, adds to the general setting by giving the peruser the data expected to explore the scholarly territory. The cautious game plan of data and the foundation of an unmistakable and cognizant structure are fundamental in guaranteeing that the peruser can understand the creator's thought process and value the commitments of the work.

Past writing and the scholarly world, setting the stage is a principal part of influential composition. Whether creating a discourse, a commentary, or a showcasing pitch, the creator should handily approach the issue, present the specific situation, and lay out the stakes to put forth a convincing defense. This includes grasping the crowd's point of view, recognizing possible counterarguments, and decisively picking the language and tone to get the ideal reaction. In a powerful setting of the stage, the creator becomes both a narrator and a rhetorician, winding around a story that catches the crowd's consideration and convinces them to see the issue from a specific vantage point.

Moreover, the setting of the stage is definitely not a one-size-fits-all undertaking; it expects flexibility to the particular requests of the class, crowd, and reason. In a secret novel, for example, setting the stage might include making a quality of tension and uncertainty, captivating the peruser to unwind the mystery close by the characters. Conversely, an enlightening paper might require an unmistakable and clear setting of the stage, introducing current realities and setting in a way that works with understanding without pointless embellishments.

Setting the stage is likewise about laying out an agreement of trust between the creator and the crowd. It includes indicating to the peruser that the creator is a proficient and dependable aide through the scholarly or innovative territory going to be crossed. This is especially pertinent in scholarly composition, where the writer's mastery and believability assume a pivotal part in forming the peruser's trust in the contentions introduced. The stage-setting turns into a chance for the creator to exhibit their dominance of the topic, giving a strong groundwork whereupon the ensuing examination or story can unfurl.

In the advanced age, where data is bountiful and abilities to focus are momentary, the specialty of setting the stage has taken on new aspects. Writers should battle with the test of catching and keeping up with the peruser's consideration in the midst of an ocean of interruptions. This requests not just clearness and brevity in that frame of mind of data yet in addition a comprehension of the visual and sight and sound components that can upgrade the setting. Whether through very much created visuals, intuitive components, or convincing narrating strategies, the computerized setting of the stage requires a combination of conventional scholarly abilities with contemporary media proficiency.

As the stage is set, the characters take their places, and the account unfurls, the underlying basis laid by the creator starts to prove to be fruitful. The peruser, whether exploring the exciting bends in the road of a novel, understanding the coherent movement of a scholarly contention, or being convinced by a convincing paper, depends on the establishment laid out in the setting of the stage to figure out the unfurling talk. The craft of setting the stage, thusly, isn't simply a preface yet a basic piece of the whole savvy or inventive excursion.

All in all, setting the stage is a complex and dynamic cycle that reaches out across different types of talk. It includes portraying the actual environmental elements as well as drenching the crowd in the worldly, social, and profound scene. Whether in writing, the scholarly community, or convincing composition, the setting of the stage is an essential move by the writer to lay out setting, outline the story, and get a specific reaction from the crowd.

In the computerized age, the difficulties and amazing open doors in setting the stage have extended, requesting versatility and advancement to catch and keep up with the peruser's consideration. As the drapery rises, the stage set by the creator turns into the material whereupon the scholarly or inventive work of art unfurls.

1.2 Brief history of football

A Concise History of Football:

Football, known as soccer in certain districts to recognize it from American and Canadian football, is a game that has caught the hearts and minds of millions around the world. Established in old civic establishments and developing through hundreds of years, football has become something beyond a game; a worldwide peculiarity rises above social and geological limits. As we set out on an excursion through the records of history, we find the intriguing development of football, from its initial simple structures to the coordinated and profoundly serious game we know today.

The starting points of football can be followed back to antiquated human advancements, where different societies participated in ball games that bore likenesses to the cutting edge sport. In China during the Han Line (206 BCE - 220 CE), a game called "cuju" involved players kicking a cowhide ball through an opening in a silk fabric hung between two bamboo posts. Likewise, the Greeks and Romans participated in ball games, with the Romans embracing a rendition called "harpastum." These old ball games laid the preparation for what might ultimately become football, with normal components like kicking, passing, and scoring objectives.

As history unfurled, various areas fostered their own varieties of football-like games. In archaic Europe, especially in Britain, different types of football arose. These games were in many cases tumultuous and needed normalized rules, prompting continuous conflicts among players and networks. One outstanding variant, known as "crowd football," involved mass support, little association, and frequently brought about raucous and vicious way of behaving. The absence of normalized rules and broad varieties implied that every local area had its own rendition of football, making it trying to lay out an all inclusive structure for the game.

The defining moment in the development of football accompanied the rise of schools and colleges in archaic Britain. These instructive establishments assumed a significant part in classifying the guidelines and making a normalized form of the game. In any case, the guidelines were a long way from uniform across schools, prompting proceeded with varieties. One essential arrangement of rules was created at Rugby School in the mid nineteenth hundred years, accentuating conveying the ball and handling adversaries. This rendition of football established the groundwork for what might ultimately become rugby football, a particular game from affiliation football (soccer).

The requirement for normalized rules and an all inclusive structure turned out to be more evident as football kept on acquiring fame. In 1863, a pivotal turning point throughout the entire existence of football happened with the foundation of the Football Affiliation (FA) in Britain. The FA met delegates from different clubs and schools to make a normalized set of rules, known as the Laws of the Game. These guidelines framed basic standards like the utilization of a round ball, the restriction of utilizing hands (with the exception of the goalkeeper), and the idea of an objective scored by driving the ball into the rival's objective.

The foundation of normalized rules by the Football Affiliation denoted the conventional partition between affiliation football and rugby football. The expression "soccer" itself has its underlying foundations in Britain, got from "relationship." While the normalized rules gave an establishment to the cutting edge game, local varieties endured, and football kept on developing diversely in different regions of the planet.

Football immediately spread past the shores of Britain, tracking down ripe ground in other European nations and South America. The globalization of the game was worked with by elements like worldwide exchange, expansionism, and the impact of English exiles. The principal worldwide football match occurred in 1872 among Britain and Scotland, laying the foundation for the advancement of global contests.

The late nineteenth and mid twentieth hundreds of years saw the formalization of football administration at the global level. In 1904, the Fédération Internationale de Football Affiliation (FIFA) was established in Paris, uniting football relationship from a few nations. FIFA's job was to manage and sort out worldwide contests, encouraging cooperation and normalization in the worldwide football local area. The debut FIFA World Cup occurred in Uruguay in 1930, denoting the start of a practice that would charm the world like clockwork.

As football acquired ubiquity around the world, it confronted difficulties and went through changes intelligent of the socio-political scene. The game turned into a wellspring of public pride and personality, with matches taking on representative importance. During times of contention and war, football filled in as a bringing together power, giving comfort and brotherhood in the midst of misfortune. On the other hand, football additionally experienced occasions where political strains spilled onto the field, as seen in scandalous matches during the Virus War period.

The post-The Second Great War time frame saw a flood in the globalization of football, with clubs and players accomplishing worldwide praise. The coming of broadcast communicates brought the game into lounges all over the planet, raising football to extraordinary degrees of notoriety.

The 1950s and 1960s saw the ascent of famous players like Pelé and Diego Maradona, who became inseparable from the excellence and expertise of the game.

The twentieth century likewise saw the rise of mainland club contests, for example, the UEFA Champions Association in Europe and the Copa Libertadores in South America. These contests added one more layer of energy and notoriety to football, exhibiting the best clubs and players from various districts. The convergence of business sponsorships and media freedoms further moved football into the domain of enormous business, changing it into an extravagant industry.

The turn of the thousand years brought new difficulties and open doors for football. Mechanical progressions, especially in correspondence and broadcasting, permitted fans to associate with the game on a worldwide scale. The web, virtual entertainment, and web based streaming stages reformed the manner in which fans consumed football, separating geological obstructions and making a really worldwide fan local area.

All the while, the commercialization of football raised worries about issues like monetary disparity, debasement, and the commodification of the game. The cosmic exchange charges and pay rates directed by top players, combined with the monetary tensions looked by clubs, prompted banters about the maintainability and morals of current football. Issues like prejudice, segregation, and match-fixing additionally presented huge difficulties to the game's honesty.

Because of these difficulties, football overseeing bodies and partners have looked to resolve issues like monetary fair play, variety and consideration, and moral lead. The game has turned into a stage for social change, with players and associations upholding for purposes like enemy of bigotry, orientation correspondence, and ecological maintainability.

As we stand at the edge of another time, football keeps on advancing, mirroring the powerful transaction among custom and development. The game's capacity to adjust to changing times while saving its center substance is a demonstration of its persevering through bid. From its unassuming starting points on shoddy fields to the loftiness of current arenas, football has risen above its status as a simple game to turn into a social peculiarity that joins individuals across landmasses.

All in all, the historical backdrop of football is an embroidery woven with strings of old ball games, middle age varieties, and the formalization of rules in nineteenth century Britain. The foundation of normalized rules by the Football Affiliation, the production of FIFA, and the approach of worldwide rivalries checked key achievements in the worldwide development of the game.

Football's excursion through the twentieth century saw it become a social peculiarity, with famous players, worldwide contests, and a huge worldwide fan base. The 21st century has brought new difficulties and open doors, with innovation, commercialization, and social issues forming the cutting edge football scene. As the game keeps on catching the hearts of millions, its rich history fills in as a demonstration of the persevering through influence of football to move, join together, and rise above borders.

1.3 The universal appeal of the game
The General Allure of the Game:

Football, known as soccer in many regions of the planet, has a general allure that rises above social, topographical, and phonetic limits. A game joins individuals from different foundations, giving a typical language that encourages kinship and shared encounters. The general allure of football can be credited to a few elements, going from its straightforwardness and openness to its capacity to bring out energy, make networks, and act as a stage for social trade.

At its center, football is a straightforward game that requires insignificant gear - a ball and an open space. This straightforwardness is a critical consider its worldwide ubiquity, as it makes the game open to individuals of any age, sexual orientations, and monetary foundations. Whether played in the dusty roads of a favela in Brazil, on a fix of grass in a rural area, or in a cutting edge arena in Europe, the essential substance of the game remaining parts unaltered. This openness has added to football's capacity to saturate each side of the globe, turning into an omnipresent and comprehensive hobby.

The comprehensiveness of football is likewise obvious in its ability to summon energy and feeling. Seeing an impeccably executed objective, the show of a punishment shootout, or the euphoria of dominating an essential game produces an instinctive reaction that rises above phonetic and social contrasts. The general language of festivity, dissatisfaction, and celebration spoken on football fields all over the planet permits fans to interface with the game on a profoundly close to home level. The common experience of watching or playing football makes a feeling of having a place and family relationship among fans, cultivating a worldwide local area that commends the ups and perseveres through the downs together.

Networks structure around football, both locally and worldwide, making a feeling of character and having a place. Nearby football clubs become the point of convergence of networks, with allies shaping a bond that stretches out past the hour and a half of a match. These clubs become a fundamental piece of the social texture, addressing something beyond a games group.

They epitomize the aggregate character and goals of a local area, giving a wellspring of pride and shared history. The worldwide football local area, incorporating fans from each side of the world, further builds up the feeling of having a place, as allies interface with similar devotees on a common excursion of wins and hardships.

The worldwide allure of football is amplified by the assorted exhibit of playing styles, strategies, and customs that various countries bring to the game. The game fills in as a stage for social trade, permitting fans to appreciate and embrace the novel flavors every nation adds to the footballing embroidery. From the samba-imbued style of Brazilian football to the trained strategic methodology of Italian groups, the variety inside the game enhances its worldwide allure. Global contests, like the FIFA World Cup and mainland competitions, exhibit this rich woven artwork, welcoming fans to submerge themselves in the stories and narratives of countries from the perspective of football.

Also, football has the ability to rise above political and social divisions, uniting individuals in snapshots of solidarity and fortitude. Verifiable models flourish, for example, the Christmas Détente of 1914 during The Second Great War while restricting troopers played football in a dead zone, saving threats briefly of shared mankind. All the more as of late, cases of football filling in as an impetus for harmony and compromise have been seen in struggle ridden districts. The game's capacity to slice through political contrasts and encourage shared understanding highlights its true capacity as a power for positive change.

The comprehensiveness of football is additionally intensified by its status as a worldwide exhibition. Significant competitions, like the FIFA World Cup, draw in a viewership that outperforms the limits of individual countries. Billions of individuals check out watch the show unfurl, by and large encountering the ups and downs of the competition. The worldwide idea of football occasions changes them into shared social minutes, with fans from various landmasses participating in conversations, discussions, and festivities. This common experience, worked with by present day correspondence innovations, makes a feeling of worldwide fellowship that is one of a kind to the universe of football.

As football keeps on advancing in the computerized age, the general allure of the game tracks down new roads of articulation. Web-based entertainment stages give a virtual space to fans to interface, share their energy, and partake in worldwide discussions about the game. The promptness of data and the openness of features empower fans to draw in with the worldwide football local area continuously, separating transient and spatial boundaries. The computerized period has democratized admittance to football content, permitting fans to add to the account of the game in manners that were beforehand unbelievable.

The comprehensiveness of football, be that as it may, doesn't mean a one-size-fits-all experience. The excellence of the game lies in its capacity to oblige and embrace variety. From the grassroots level, where nearby varieties and customs shape the game, to the zenith of expert football, where different playing ways of thinking combine, football obliges a range of styles and approaches. This adaptability adds to the game's getting through importance and flexibility across societies and ages.

While praising the general allure of football, it is pivotal to recognize the difficulties and discussions that go with the game. Issues like prejudice, separation, debasement, and monetary lopsided characteristics have damaged football's picture and brought up issues about its moral aspects. The game's capacity to address and defeat these difficulties will be critical in guaranteeing that its general allure stays a positive and comprehensive power.

All in all, the general allure of football is a demonstration of the game's capacity to rise above obstructions and associate individuals on a worldwide scale. From its modest starting points as a basic game played in different settings to its ongoing status as a social peculiarity with billions of fans, football's process mirrors the common human experience. The game's openness, close to home reverberation, ability to make networks, and job as a stage for social trade add to its general charm. As football keeps on enamoring hearts all over the planet, its capacity to motivate, join together, and encourage a feeling of having a place builds up its status as the world's generally dearest game.

CHAPTER 2

Birth of AmbitionThe Introduction of Aspiration:

Desire, the persistent quest for individual and expert objectives, is a main impetus that moves people to defeat difficulties, jump all over chances, and take a stab at significance. The introduction of desire is a mind boggling exchange of inside factors, outer impacts, and the unique powers that shape a singular's personality and yearnings. From the earliest notions of desire in youth to the experienced and nuanced structures it takes in adulthood, the excursion of aspiration is an enthralling investigation of human potential, inspiration, and strength.

At its commencement, desire frequently grows in the prolific soil of young life dreams and yearnings. The youthful brain, untethered by the requirements of the real world, imagines a heap of conceivable outcomes. Whether energized by natural gifts, early impacts, or sheer interest, youngsters start to figure out a feeling of what they need to accomplish throughout everyday life.

These incipient desires are frequently portrayed by effortlessness and honesty, going from fantasies about turning into a space explorer, a fireman, or a superhuman. The seeds of desire established in youth establish the groundwork for the goals that will shape a singular's direction in the years to come.

As people change from youth to immaturity, the thriving feeling of desire goes through a transformation. The impact of schooling, cultural assumptions, and friend communications starts to shape and refine the forms of desire. Scholarly accomplishments, extracurricular pursuits, and individual interests add to the developing account of what one tries to turn into. The teen years are set apart by a sensitive dance between self-revelation and outside assumptions, as people explore the maze of decisions that will influence their future desires.

The cultural and social milieu wherein an individual is implanted assumes a vital part in molding the nature and force of desire. Societies that celebrate independence and enterprising soul might cultivate aspirations of development, authority, or imaginative articulation. On the other hand, social orders with areas of strength for an on custom and congruity might channel desires toward laid out ways of progress, like proficient professions or scholarly accomplishments. The interchange between social qualities and individual yearnings adds layers of intricacy to the introduction of desire, featuring the complicated dance between the individual and their current circumstance.

Schooling, as a strong molding force, turns into a pot for desire during early stages. Schools and colleges act as hatcheries where desire is tried, refined, and some of the time reclassified. The quest for information, openness to assorted disciplines, and cooperations with tutors and friends add to the development of desire. The scholastic climate, with its difficulties and potential open doors, turns into a rich ground where people improve their abilities, defy mishaps, and develop the flexibility that is natural for aggressive pursuits.

The rise of desire isn't bound to the scholastic domain alone; it reaches out into the domain of individual interests and interests. Side interests, imaginative pursuits, and extracurricular exercises become labs where people explore different avenues regarding their aspirations. Whether it's the hopeful craftsman going through endless hours idealizing their art, the growing researcher directing trials in a stopgap lab, or the hopeful competitor pushing the limits of actual perseverance, these pursuits add to the diverse idea of desire. The union of individual interests and intrinsic gifts frequently solidifies into a more engaged and intentional type of desire during immaturity and early adulthood.

The change to adulthood proclaims another section in the excursion of desire. As people leave on their expert and individual ways, the desires that once stewed behind the scenes become the overwhelming focus.

The quest for a profession, the longing for monetary solidness, and the mission for individual satisfaction become predominant topics. Desire, presently prepared with the real factors of the grown-up world, requires a recalibration that offsets optimism with sober mindedness. The early expert encounters, mentorship, and openness to the complexities of the picked field add to the refinement of desire, molding it into a more nuanced and informed force.

Aspiration in adulthood is frequently entwined with the quest for progress and acknowledgment. Whether in the corporate field, imaginative pursuits, or pioneering tries, people endeavor to make some meaningful difference and cut a specialty for themselves. The desire to accomplish significance, but characterized, turns into a main thrust that moves people to conquer obstructions, climate mishaps, and persevere even with difficulties. The narratives of effective people frequently uncover an ongoing idea of steadfast desire, energized by a determined quest for objectives and a refusal to make due with unremarkableness.

The introduction of desire is certainly not a static occasion; it is a continuous interaction described by variation and development. As people explore the exciting bends in the road of life, their desires go through changes impacted by evolving needs, encounters, and outer conditions. The aggressive quest for vocation objectives may, at a specific crossroads, give way to the desire for individual satisfaction, significant connections, or cultural effect. The pliability of aspiration mirrors the unique idea of human development and advancement.

In any case, the excursion of aspiration isn't without any trace of difficulties. Desire, if uncontrolled, can transform into a blade that cuts both ways, prompting burnout, lopsided characteristics, or a nearsighted spotlight on progress to the detriment of prosperity. Finding some kind of harmony among desire and balanced living requires contemplation, mindfulness, and an acknowledgment of the all encompassing nature of progress. The introduction of a sound and maintainable desire includes understanding that achievement is certainly not a direct way however a complex embroidery that incorporates self-awareness, connections, and a feeling of direction.

The cultural accounts around desire additionally add to its perplexing embroidery. Socially implanted ideas of achievement, orientation jobs, and cultural assumptions can shape the desires people feel qualified for seek after. Breaking liberated from restricting stories and cultivating a comprehensive and different comprehension of desire is urgent for establishing a strong climate where people are enabled to investigate a wide range of goals.

Desire, when bridled successfully, can be a strong power for positive change. It can possibly drive development, rouse aggregate activity, and fuel progress on both individual and cultural levels. The narratives of people who have outfit their aspiration for charity, civil rights, or ecological manageability feature the extraordinary force of desire when lined up with respectable aims.

The introduction of a socially cognizant desire grows the story past private achievement, implanting it with a feeling of obligation and a promise to adding to everyone's benefit.

All in all, the introduction of desire is a mind boggling and complex excursion that unfurls across the phases of life. From the blameless dreams of life as a youngster to the nuanced yearnings of adulthood, desire develops in light of inner and outer impacts. The interaction between private interests, cultural assumptions, instructive encounters, and social qualities shapes the direction of aspiration.

As people explore the powerful scene of desire, they experience difficulties, mishaps, and snapshots of self-revelation. The extraordinary capability of desire lies in private accomplishment as well as in its ability to drive positive change, encourage development, and add to the prosperity of people and society at large. Understanding and sustaining the introduction of desire is, in this manner, a significant investigation of human potential and the persevering quest for significant objectives.

2.1 Early Inspirations

Early Motivations:

In the mind boggling woven artwork of human turn of events, the seeds of motivation are much of the time planted in the ripe soil of early encounters, molding the direction of people and impacting their interests, yearnings, and perspective. From the delicate long periods of life as a youngster to the developmental phases of youthfulness, early motivations act as the bedrock whereupon the groundwork of character and potential is laid. This investigation digs into the bunch manners by which early motivations, whether familial, instructive, or social, employ a significant impact in chiseling the personalities and desires of people.

The family, as the main cauldron of human connection, assumes a critical part in supporting early motivations. The elements inside the nuclear family, the qualities ingrained by guardians or watchmen, and the openness to different encounters inside the family add to molding the beginning perspective of a youngster. Guardians, as the essential forces to be reckoned with during the early years, become courses of motivation through their activities, values, and support. The sustaining climate of a strong family can light the fire of interest, impart an affection for learning, and cultivate a feeling of safety that enables kids to investigate their inclinations and goals.

Instructive encounters during the early stages become ripe ground for early motivations to flourish. Instructors, colleagues, and the scholastic climate add to forming a kid's impression of the world and their own true capacity. A gifted and energetic instructor can be an impetus for motivation, lighting an affection for a specific subject or ingraining a feeling of miracle about the world. Instructive establishments that give a different and invigorating educational program offer kids the chance to investigate a scope of interests, cultivating a feeling of interest that can develop into long lasting interests.

Social impacts, including writing, craftsmanship, music, and media, assume a critical part in molding early motivations. Stories, whether passed on through books, films, or oral practices, have the ability to spellbind youthful personalities, offering looks into changed universes, viewpoints, and conceivable outcomes. Openness to different types of imaginative articulation, from compositions to music, acquaints youngsters with the lavishness of human innovativeness, extending their viewpoints and igniting likely interests. The social milieu where a youngster is submerged adds to the development of their personality and gives a material whereupon early motivations are painted.

Besides, early motivations frequently manifest as good examples — people whose accomplishments, values, or character qualities resound profoundly with a kid. These good examples can be tracked down inside the family, local area, or the more extensive open arena. A parent succeeding in a specific calling, a local area pioneer supporting for positive change, or a verifiable figure whose achievements are commended can act as wellsprings of motivation that shape a youngster's desires. The copying of respected characteristics or accomplishments of good examples turns into a directing power that impacts individuals decisions as they explore their own ways.

The normal world, with its marvels and secrets, fills in as an early motivation that starts a feeling of wonder and interest. Investigations in nature, whether through open air exercises, untamed life experiences, or logical perceptions, develop an association with the climate. This association can turn into a well-spring of motivation, lighting intrigues in fields like science, ecological science, or protection. The investigation of nature during youth encourages a feeling of stewardship and a guarantee to understanding and safeguarding the planet.

Early motivations are not bound to positive encounters alone; difficulties and misfortunes experienced during youth can likewise shape the course of one's life. The versatility exhibited even with troubles, the illustrations gained from mishaps, and the assurance to defeat impediments become strong wellsprings of motivation. Misfortunes, when explored with mental fortitude and constancy, add to the improvement of strength, genius, and a feeling of direction that can drive people to seek after aggressive objectives.

In the domain of sports, early openness to athletic exercises can act as a strong wellspring of motivation. Whether it's a youngster seeing an undeniably exhilarating game, partaking in coordinated sports, or loving a games figure, the universe of games can impart values like cooperation, discipline, and persistence. Early encounters in sports establish the groundwork for actual wellness, mental versatility, and an energy for rivalry that can reach out into adulthood, molding both sporting pursuits and expert desires.

The impact of innovation in the cutting edge time acquaints another aspect with early motivations. The computerized scene, with its huge range of data, intuitive stages, and instructive assets, offers youngsters uncommon chances to investigate different interests. From coding to virtual investigation of verifiable destinations, innovation opens ways to a universe of information and conceivable outcomes, turning into a course for early motivations in fields connected with science, innovation, designing, expressions, and math (STEAM).

As kids progress into immaturity, the seeds of early motivations planted during their early stages start to grow, taking on additional characterized shapes and headings. Youthfulness is a period set apart by self-disclosure, character development, and the investigation of individual interests and gifts. The early motivations that have flourished impact the options people make with respect to scholarly pursuits, extracurricular exercises, and potential profession ways. The interests fueled in youth develop into additional conscious pursuits, directing people toward areas of study or employments that line up with their initial motivations.

The investigation of early motivations reaches out past individual improvement to cultural ramifications. A general public that qualities and supports the different motivations of its childhood is probably going to profit from a rich embroidery of gifts, thoughts, and developments. Schooling systems that focus on comprehensive turn of events, social establishments that praise inventiveness, and networks that give open doors to different encounters add to encouraging an age of people whose early motivations bloom into commitments that improve the aggregate human experience.

Nonetheless, it is fundamental to perceive that early motivations are not static; they develop and adjust as people develop, learn, and experience the world. The underlying flash of motivation might prompt the disclosure of new interests, interests, and livelihoods that were not clear during youth. The excursion of self-disclosure is dynamic, and people frequently find motivation in surprising spots or encounters as they explore the intricacies of immaturity and adulthood.

All in all, the introduction of early motivations denotes the beginning of a deep rooted excursion of self-revelation and self-awareness. From the family climate to instructive encounters, social impacts, and experiences with good examples, the wellsprings of motivation during youth establish the groundwork for individual yearnings and interests. The complex idea of early motivations mirrors the mind boggling interchange between inward tendencies and outside impacts.

As people change into youthfulness and adulthood, the seeds of early motivations flourish, forming scholarly and vocation decisions, special goals, and the general direction of their lives. Understanding and esteeming the meaning of early motivations is vital to cultivating a general public that sustains the different likely inborn in each person.

1. **Childhood stories of legendary players**
   Youth Accounts of Unbelievable Players:
   In the rich embroidery of sports history, the youth accounts of unbelievable players frequently act as convincing stories that enlighten the ways these symbols took from humble starting points to the apexes of accomplishment. Behind the excitement and charm of arenas, prizes, and overall applause lie stories of commitment, versatility, and the unstoppable soul that characterizes wearing significance. Investigating the youth accounts of unbelievable players offers a brief look into the early stages that molded their personality, touched off their enthusiasm for the game, and laid the basis for phenomenal professions.
   Perhaps of the most notable figure throughout the entire existence of b-ball, Michael Jordan's young life story is carved in the archives of sports folklore. Brought into the world in Brooklyn, New York, in 1963, Jordan's initial years were set apart by a cutthroat soul that appeared in his persevering quest for greatness on the ball court. His dad, James Jordan Sr., perceived the prospering ability in youthful Michael and assumed a

significant part in sustaining his adoration for the game. In secondary school, Jordan confronted difficulties, at first being disregarded for the varsity group, yet his relentless assurance and hard working attitude ultimately pushed him to turn into a headliner. These early stages established the groundwork for a vocation that would see him become a six-time NBA champion, five-time MVP, and a worldwide ball symbol.

In the domain of football, the youth story of Pelé, the Brazilian legend, is a demonstration of the extraordinary force of ability and assurance. Conceived Edson Arantes do Nascimento in 1940, in the neediness stricken locale of Três Corações, Brazil, Pelé's initial openness to football came through playing with a stopgap ball made from clothes. His expertise and energy grabbed the eye of nearby club Santos, and at 15 years old, he made his expert introduction. Pelé's ascent to noticeable quality was fleeting; he drove Brazil to three World Cup triumphs and turned into the untouched driving scorer for Santos and the Brazilian public group. The devastated kid from Três Corações turned into a worldwide football minister, exhibiting the widespread allure of the game and motivating ages of players.

The domain of tennis brags one the most getting through youth stories as Serena and Venus Williams. Brought up in Compton, California, in the midst of a scenery of financial difficulties and posse viciousness, the Williams sisters arose as tennis wonders under the direction of their dad, Richard Williams. Richard, regardless of having no conventional preparation in tennis, made a 78-page plan for the expert tennis progress of his little girls before they were even conceived. The sisters went through thorough preparation on open tennis courts, with Serena, specifically, displaying a crude ability that would later see her become one of the best tennis players ever. The Williams sisters' experience growing up story is an account of versatility, familial help, and an enduring faith in the force of dreams.

Moving to the universe of cricket, the youth story of Sachin Tendulkar, frequently alluded to as the "Little Expert," is a demonstration of the getting through effect of energy and commitment. Brought into the world in Mumbai, India, in 1973, Tendulkar's relationship with cricket started at a young age. His senior sibling, Ajit, perceived Sachin's ability right off the bat and urged him to seek after the game. Tendulkar's cricketing venture took a crucial turn when he was trained by Ramakant Achrekar, who might frequently offer him a coin for each meeting in which he didn't get out. The notorious picture of a youthful Tendulkar rehearsing with a solitary stump and a cricket ball fastened to a string catches the pith of his unassuming starting points. From those early days, Tendulkar proceeded to turn into the most elevated run-scorer in global cricket, acquiring applause in India as well as across the cricketing scene.

The universe of games is decorated with the motivating youth story of Usain Bolt, the Jamaican runner generally viewed as the quickest man ever. Brought into the world in the provincial town of Sherwood Content in 1986, Bolt's normal ability for running was obvious since early on. His initial years were set apart by a rich love for sports, with cricket and football at first catching his advantage. In any case, it was his huge speed on the track that accumulated consideration. Bolt's excursion from the country fields of Jamaica to the world stage unfurled with a progression of record-breaking runs, coming full circle in his notorious exhibitions at the 2008 Beijing Olympics, where he set worldwide bests in the 100m and 200m runs. Bolt's experience growing up story mirrors the effect of crude ability, combined with a light soul and a persistent quest for greatness.

In the realm of golf, the youth story of Tiger Woods is inseparable from tremendous ability, tireless desire, and noteworthy achievement. Brought into the world in Cypress, California, in 1975, Woods showed an early partiality for golf, sharpened by his dad, Baron Woods, a resigned armed force lieutenant colonel. Lord acquainted Tiger with golf before he turned two, and the youthful wonder was soon displaying his abilities on TV syndicated programs.

Woods' predominance started during his beginner years, winning three back to back U.S. Junior Novice titles. His change to the expert circuit denoted a change in perspective in golf, as Woods proceeded to become quite possibly of the best and persuasive competitor throughout the entire existence of the game.

These youth stories highlight normal subjects that rise above the particular games and foundations of these incredible players. Family assumes an essential part, with strong guardians perceiving and supporting early indications of ability. The impact of mentors and tutors arises as an ongoing idea, directing these youthful competitors through the intricacies of their picked sports. Moreover, the early stages of these unbelievable players are set apart by a blend of difficulties and wins, mishaps and triumphs, making a pot that produces character, flexibility, and a steady quest for significance.

Past the singular stories, the shared characteristic of these youth accounts lies in the groundbreaking force of game itself. Sports become a method for actual articulation as well as a vehicle for self-improvement, self-revelation, and the development of values like discipline, collaboration, and persistence. The youth accounts of unbelievable players motivate hopeful competitors as well as impact anybody taking a stab at greatness in their picked field.

Also, the effect of these players stretches out past the domains of sports.

They become social symbols, breaking hindrances, testing standards, and filling in as images of motivation for people from different foundations. The youth accounts of these legends become piece of the aggregate story, showing that significance is many times brought into the world in the pot of affliction, molded by early impacts, and filled by a resolute obligation to understanding one's true capacity.

As these amazing players describe their initial encounters, they frequently accentuate the job of enthusiasm and love for the game as the main thrust behind their prosperity. The delight and excitement they found in their experience growing up pursuits established the groundwork for long lasting responsibilities to their separate games. The straightforwardness of playing for the love of the game, whether on stopgap fields, public tennis courts, or nearby b-ball courts, turns into a repetitive subject in their stories.

In the contemporary period, where pro athletics have become multimillion-dollar enterprises, the youth accounts of unbelievable players likewise act as a wake up call of the immaculateness of game in its substance. It is an update that underneath the business supports, arena lights, and worldwide show, there exists a kid who became hopelessly enamored with a game and committed themselves to understanding their fantasies.

All in all, the youth accounts of unbelievable players are spellbinding stories that rise above the limits of sports. They are stories of enthusiasm, devotion, and the extraordinary force of early motivations. From the ball courts of Brooklyn to the cricket fields of Mumbai, these accounts offer looks into the early stages that molded famous professions. The consistent ideas of familial help, mentorship, versatility, and an unfaltering adoration for the game weave a story that reverberates with hopeful competitors and fans the same. These youth stories act as a demonstration of the getting through effect of sports on self-improvement, the quest for greatness, and the immortal charm of the games that dazzle hearts all over the planet.

2. **First encounters with a football**

First Experiences with a Football:

The principal experience with a football is a transitional experience that rises above social, topographical, and financial limits. For some people, this prologue to the circular item that holds the commitment of vast conceivable outcomes addresses the inception into a universe of fellowship, rivalry, and shared happiness. Whether the setting is a metropolitan jungle gym, a dusty town field, or a manicured rural grass, the reverberation of that underlying collaboration with a football reverberations all through a lifetime, making a permanent imprint on the individual and frequently forming a long lasting relationship with the delightful game.

In the easiest of terms, a football is a sewed circle of cowhide or engineered material, expanded with air, yet its importance goes a long ways past its actual piece. It is an image of solidarity, an impetus for kinships, and a vessel for dreams. The primary experience with a football is a tangible encounter - the particular smell of cowhide, an impeccably struck ball, the material vibe of its surface against one's skin - all add to a vivid commencement into a world that rises above the everyday and opens up a range of potential outcomes.

For some, the primary experience with a football happens in youth, when the world is seen from the perspective of marvel and investigation. It very well may be a more established kin acquainting the more youthful one with the nuts and bolts of passing and shooting, a parent starting a round of catch in the terrace, or an unconstrained kickabout with companions in the area. No matter what the unique circumstance, the principal bit of a football is many times a snapshot of disclosure, a prologue to a motor language that talks across societies and ages.

In metropolitan scenes, where open spaces are a superior, the roads act as the primary pitch for endless yearning footballers. The clacking hints of a ball bobbing against concrete, the unrehearsed goal lines set apart by disposed of coats, and the clamor of energized voices structure the scenery of these early football experiences.

In these conditions, football turns out to be in excess of a game; it turns into a method for self-articulation, a departure from the imperatives of metropolitan life, and a wellspring of unrestrained delight. The substantial wilderness changes into a field of dreams, with each kick of the ball addressing a snapshot of freedom and plausibility.

Conversely, provincial settings offer an alternate background for the primary experiences with a football. Open fields, frequently lopsided and sketchy, become the material for improvised matches. The barefooted kid, with a ball at their feet, figures out how to explore the knocks and fissure of the landscape, fostering a special association with the game. The limits are inexactly characterized, and the goal lines may be set apart by stones or sticks, however the substance of football stays unaltered - a shared encounter that rises above the impediments of assets.

Rural areas give a center ground, frequently highlighting very much manicured yards and coordinated sports associations. In these settings, the principal experiences with a football might be more organized, with guardians selecting their kids in youth associations or coordinating end of the week matches in local area parks. The charm of group activities, the excitement of rivalry, and the kinship shaped on these rural fields add to a nuanced prologue to football, where the game turns into a social paste that ties networks together.

The principal bit of a football isn't just an actual cooperation; an inception into a culture traverses the globe. Football is a language expressed by millions, a social peculiarity that extensions separates and makes a common encounter. The principal experience with a football is frequently joined by openness to the more extensive footballing world - famous players, incredible matches, and the display of significant competitions. The youngster kicking a ball in a dusty rear entryway could fantasy about imitating their most loved footballing legend, and in that fantasy, the limits of geology and situation break down.

The grassroots idea of football, obvious in these underlying experiences, is a demonstration of the game's vote based bid. Dissimilar to a few different games that require particular hardware or offices, everything necessary for a round of football is a ball and a space to play. This openness is a significant calculate football's all inclusive prevalence, permitting it to rise above financial hindrances and become a game individuals. The primary experience with a football, no matter what the setting, establishes the groundwork for this openness, making the game a popularity based pursuit that invites members from varying backgrounds.

The meaning of the primary experience with a football reaches out past the quick rush of kicking a ball. It denotes the start of an excursion - an excursion of expertise improvement, kinship, and self-improvement. As people progress from those underlying kicks to additional organized types of play, whether in school groups or neighborhood clubs, the football turns into a dependable friend, a steadfast accomplice chasing dominance over the game. The simple abilities mastered during those early experiences - the specialty of spilling, the accuracy of passing, the excitement of scoring - develop into a nuanced comprehension of the game.

The main experiences with a football are frequently worked with by tutors - more seasoned kin, companions, guardians, or mentors - who share their affection for the game and give direction. These tutors become the guardians of football shrewdness, passing down specialized abilities as well as the elusive characteristics that characterize a genuine footballer - versatility, cooperation, discipline, and an affection for the wonderful game. The mentorship dynamic laid out during these early experiences adds to the social texture of football, where information is shared, and the delight of the game is gone down through ages.

In schools, the principal experiences with a football are many times organized inside actual training programs or coordinated sports exercises. The rectangular schoolyard, with goal lines at one or the flip side, turns into a smaller than normal arena where youngsters gain proficiency with the guidelines, foster collaboration abilities, and participate in cordial contest. These early encounters in coordinated settings lay the basis for the improvement of a long lasting energy for football. Schools become hatcheries for ability, sustaining the up and coming age of players and aficionados who will convey the adoration for the game into their grown-up lives.

The orientation aspect of the primary experiences with a football has developed over the long run. By and large, football has been transcendently related with male cooperation, yet a developing acknowledgment of orientation equity in sports has prompted expanded open doors for young ladies to draw in with the game. Seeing young ladies kicking a ball in schoolyards, joining youth groups, and taking part in coordinated associations mirrors a positive change in cultural perspectives toward ladies' contribution in football. The principal experiences with a football for some young ladies connote an individual inception into the game as well as a separating of orientation generalizations and the declaration of their entitlement to play.

The progress from these early, unstructured experiences with a football to more formalized interest frequently includes joining neighborhood clubs or youth foundations. These coordinated settings give a more methodical way to deal with expertise improvement, strategic comprehension, and serious play. The fellowship shaped in these settings frequently develops into profound and enduring companionships, as people share the ups and downs of their footballing ventures. The club turns into a subsequent home, and the partners become a more distant family bound together by a common energy for the game.

The primary experiences with a football can likewise be groundbreaking surprisingly. For some's purposes, it turns into a method for social joining, particularly in multicultural settings where people from different foundations meet up through a common love for the game. The football field turns into a blend where etymological and social contrasts are saved for a typical language - the language of the delightful game. These multicultural experiences add to a rich embroidery of encounters, encouraging an appreciation for variety and solidarity through football.

The close to home reverberation of the primary experiences with a football is unmistakable in the stories of unbelievable players who follow their adoration for the game back to humble starting points. For the majority footballing symbols, the underlying kicks on improvised fields, frequently without appropriate hardware or offices, turned into the pot where their ability was found and supported. These legends frequently tell accounts of utilizing stopgap balls, playing shoeless, and exploring testing territories as they improved their abilities. The effortlessness of those early experiences shapes the establishment for the complicated and stunning abilities these players would later feature on the amazing phases of expert football.

As people progress in their footballing ventures, the primary experiences with a football keep on holding an exceptional spot in their souls. The wistfulness related with those developmental minutes turns into a wellspring of motivation, a sign of the unadulterated bliss and unrestrained energy that attracted them to the game. The sights, sounds, and feelings of those early kicks wait in the memory, turning into a wellspring of inspiration during testing times and a standard for reconnecting with the pith of the game.

The social effect of the primary experiences with a football is clear in the ceremonies and customs that encompass the game. The unconstrained kickabouts in area stops, the off the cuff matches on sea shores, and the merry environment during significant football competitions are undeniably established in the aggregate memory of those underlying connections with a football. These common encounters make a feeling of local area and having a place, encouraging a social personality that rises above individual contrasts.

The primary experiences with a football likewise mark the start of a deep rooted relationship with the game. For some, football isn't simply a side interest or a hobby; it turns into a focal component of their personality. The adoration for the game stretches out past the limits of the field, impacting way of life decisions, groups of friends, and even vocation ways. The football turns into a steady friend, a charm that represents dreams, desires, and the persevering through soul of play.

All in all, the primary experiences with a football are a general and extraordinary experience that rises above age, orientation, and foundation. Whether on dusty roads, rural yards, or schoolyards, the inception into the universe of football is set apart by a feeling of marvel, energy, and the commitment of experience. These early collaborations establish the groundwork for a long lasting relationship with the game, molding abilities and strategies as well as values, companionships, and social characters. As the ball rolls, moved by the energy of those first kicks, it conveys with it the accounts of incalculable people whose lives have been moved by the wizardry of football.

2.2 Dreams Take Shape

Dreams Come to fruition:

In the tremendous scene of human yearnings, the excursion from dream to the truth is a nuanced investigation of flexibility, assurance, and the complicated dance among desire and difficulty. The molding of dreams is a profoundly private and dynamic cycle, impacted by inside inspirations, outside conditions, and the interminable quest for one's interests. From the flash of a plan to the substantial indication of an objective, the development of dreams typifies the pith of human potential and the groundbreaking force of steadfast responsibility.

At the center of this excursion lies the initiation of a fantasy — a snapshot of motivation, a brief look at probability, or an intense longing that touches off the creative mind. Dreams, in their beginning structure, frequently rise up out of the prolific soil of individual interests, gifts, or encounters. They address the unknown regions of potential, alluring people to wander into domains where their interests meet with the vast scenes of what could be. This underlying phase of dreaming is portrayed by a feeling of marvel, interest, and the daringness to imagine real factors past the requirements of the present.

As dreams flourish, the following period of their advancement includes the sensitive interaction among vision and arranging. The shapeless forms of a fantasy start to solidify into unmistakable objectives, set apart by essential reasoning, careful preparation, and a guide for acknowledgment. This progress from deliberation to lucidity requires a mix of imagination and sober mindedness, as people explore the landscape of conceivable outcomes while establishing their goals in the reasonable items of execution. The demonstration of forming dreams includes setting feasible achievements, separating complex targets into sensible undertakings, and developing a mentality that flourishes with both desire and reasonableness.

Outer impacts assume a vital part in the development of dreams. Social, social, and ecological variables shape the direction of desires, introducing the two potential open doors and difficulties. Steady organizations, tutors, and openness to assorted viewpoints add to the refinement of dreams, offering direction and approval en route. Alternately, cultural standards, monetary circumstances, and fundamental boundaries can introduce impressive impediments that request strength and imaginative critical thinking. The molding of dreams is, subsequently, a unique discussion between inward vision and outside real factors, requiring flexibility and a readiness to explore the perplexing embroidery of impacts that shape individual directions.

The sign of dreams frequently includes a cooperative connection among schooling and self-awareness. The quest for information, whether formal or casual, turns into a foundation in the acknowledgment of goals.

Schooling not just furnishes people with the abilities and mastery expected to explore their picked ways yet in addition cultivates an outlook of consistent learning and variation. The excursion from dream to the truth is set apart by a pledge to scholarly development, a receptiveness to groundbreaking thoughts, and an acknowledgment of the extraordinary expected innate in the procurement of information.

The domain of vocation yearnings gives a powerful scenery to the investigation of how dreams come to fruition. Numerous people set out on proficient excursions driven by a dream of significant and satisfying work.

The arrangement of individual interests with proficient pursuits turns into a focal topic, as people look for vocations that reverberate with their deepest dreams and values. The forming of profession dreams includes vital decisions, expertise improvement, and frequently, an eagerness to explore unanticipated diversions or difficulties. The advancement of these yearnings mirrors the complex dance between private satisfaction and cultural assumptions, as people cut out spaces where their genuine selves can flourish.

Pioneering dreams, portrayed by the longing to make, develop, and add to the business scene, give an interesting focal point through which the molding of dreams can be inspected. The commencement of an enterprising dream frequently emerges from an apparent hole on the lookout, an enthusiasm for tackling a specific issue, or a venturesome vision of what could be. The excursion from ideation to the foundation of a business implies risk-taking, versatility notwithstanding disappointments, and a relentless confidence in the extraordinary force of one's thoughts. The molding of pioneering dreams exemplifies the combination of desire, inventiveness, and a tenacious quest for objectives that stretch out past private accomplishment to influence the more extensive monetary and social texture.

Imaginative pursuits, whether in artistic expression, writing, or different types of articulation, offer one more material for the investigation of how dreams come to fruition. The craftsman's process is in many cases set apart by a profound association with individual imagination, a longing to impart remarkable viewpoints, and a guarantee to sharpening create. The molding of imaginative dreams includes a sensitive harmony among realness and outside gathering, as makers explore the territory of self-articulation while looking for reverberation with crowds. The advancement of imaginative dreams is frequently entwined with the more extensive social scene, reflecting and molding cultural accounts all the while.

The domain of sports gives a unique field where dreams come to fruition through actual ability, discipline, and a tireless quest for greatness. Competitors, from hopeful beginners to tip top experts, set out on ventures energized by dreams of triumph, acknowledgment, and the sheer delight of pushing physical and mental limits. The molding of sports dreams includes thorough preparation, key preparation, and the development of mental strength to explore the ups and downs of serious scenes.

The quest for athletic dreams turns into a demonstration of the groundbreaking force of discipline, persistence, and the steady obligation to understanding one's true capacity.Self-improvement, including wellbeing and health, self-revelation, and the journey for a satisfying life, addresses a fundamental feature of how dreams come to fruition. The longing for comprehensive prosperity frequently ignites dreams connected with actual wellness, emotional well-being, and a feeling of direction.

The molding of these fantasies includes deliberate decisions, way of life changes, and the development of propensities that add to by and large wellbeing. The excursion toward self-awareness is a ceaseless investigation, set apart by self-reflection, versatility, and a pledge to the continuous course of turning into the best version of oneself.

The cultural effect of dreams that come to fruition is significant, affecting social stories, cultural advancement, and the aggregate creative mind.

Developments conceived out of visionary dreams, whether fixated on civil rights, natural supportability, or mechanical advancement, shape the course of history. The forming of cultural dreams includes aggregate desires, shared values, and the preparation of networks toward shared objectives. The extraordinary force of these fantasies stretches out past individual pursuits, adding to the advancement of developments and the common embroidered artwork of human experience.

Dreams frequently face the cauldron of difficulty, testing the strength and guts of the individuals who try to carry them to completion. The excursion from dream to the truth is definitely not a direct direction yet a wandering way set apart by difficulties, mishaps, and snapshots of self-question. The molding of dreams includes the route of these obstructions with beauty and assurance. It requires an outlook that sees disappointments as any open doors for development, misfortunes as impermanent diversions, and difficulties as essential parts of the extraordinary excursion.

The story of dreams coming to fruition is deficient without recognizing the job of desire — the main impetus that pushes people to arrive at past their ongoing conditions and imagine a future pervaded with plausibility. Aspiration is the heartbeat of dreams, giving the musicality that supports the excursion through its rhythmic movements. The forming of aggressive dreams includes a sensitive equilibrium, requiring a degree of dauntlessness that resists business as usual while outstanding grounded in a practical comprehension of the difficulties ahead.

As dreams come to fruition, the significance of strength arises as a common subject. The capacity to weather conditions storms, return quickly from mishaps, and continue even with difficulty is a sign of the people who own their fantasies to completion. Flexibility isn't simply a characteristic; an expertise can be developed through the affirmation of one's inward strength, a positive mentality, and a guarantee to gaining from each insight. The molding of versatile dreams includes a personal hit the dance floor with difficulties, changing obstructions into venturing stones on the way to acknowledgment.

The advancement of dreams is personally associated with the idea of character — the unfurling comprehension of what one's identity is and who one tries to turn into. Dreams frequently act as mirrors mirroring the most profound longings, values, and potential inside people.

The forming of dreams turns into an excursion of self-revelation, a cycle that includes stripping away layers of cultural molding, outside assumptions, and self-restricting convictions to uncover the valid center of one's yearnings. The arrangement of dreams with valid personality makes a strong cooperative energy, driving people toward a more certifiable and satisfying presence.

The convergence of energy and object is an essential junction in the excursion of dreams coming to fruition. Energy, the well established love for a specific pursuit, mixes energy and excitement into the molding of dreams. Reason, the feeling of importance and commitment, adds a significant aspect to goals, securing them in a more extensive setting. The arrangement of enthusiasm and reason changes dreams into vehicles for individual satisfaction and cultural effect. The molding of direction driven dreams turns into a groundbreaking demonstration, transforming individual desires into powers for positive change.

The job of tutors and good examples is instrumental in the excursion from dreaming to forming reality. Coaches give direction, intelligence, and a guide in light of their own encounters. They become guides of motivation, enlightening the way ahead and offering support during testing times. Good examples, whether genuine or optimistic, act as undeniable evidence that fantasies are achievable and that the excursion is traversable. The molding of dreams frequently includes the acknowledgment that one isn't the only one, that others have trampled comparable ways, and that achievement is certainly not a detached accomplishment yet an aggregate undertaking.

In the contemporary scene, the impact of innovation on the molding of dreams is significant. The advanced age has democratized admittance to data, assets, and stages for self-articulation. The molding of dreams in the advanced time includes utilizing innovation as an empowering agent, whether through web-based training, virtual cooperation, or the enhancement of one's voice through computerized stages. The interconnectedness worked with by innovation has changed the scene of probability, giving new roads to dreams to come to fruition and contact worldwide crowds.

All in all, the excursion from dreams coming to fruition to their unmistakable acknowledgment is a diverse investigation of human potential, strength, and the groundbreaking force of desire. The molding of dreams includes a sensitive dance between inside vision and outside real factors, a discussion with cultural impacts, and a guarantee to constant development.

As dreams develop from unique yearnings to substantial real factors, they become a demonstration of the dauntless soul of the people who set out to imagine a future past the limits of the present. The story of dreams coming to fruition is an all inclusive adventure, woven into the texture of human experience, mirroring the immortal quest for a daily existence implanted with importance, reason, and the determined quest for one's most noteworthy yearnings.

1. **Joining local youth teams**
   Joining Neighborhood Youth Groups: A Groundbreaking Excursion of Development and Enthusiasm
   The choice to join a neighborhood youth group in any wearing discipline denotes a urgent second in the existence of trying competitors. It is a

decision powered by enthusiasm, a longing for expertise improvement, and the fantasy about having a place with a local area limited by a common love for the game. The excursion from individual play to group interest addresses a critical shift, one that acquaints youthful competitors with a unique universe of brotherhood, organized preparing, and the excitement of cutthroat play. This groundbreaking experience shapes athletic capacities as well as gives significant fundamental abilities, encouraging self-awareness and strength.

Neighborhood youth groups act as hatcheries for ability, giving an organized stage to youthful competitors to improve their abilities and develop a more profound comprehension of their picked sport. The choice to join a group frequently emerges from a mix of characteristic energy and outer impacts - be it the support of family, the motivation got from sports icons, or the basic delight of playing with peers. The charm of being important for a group, where individual commitments blend into a bound together exertion, is a strong inspiration that drives youthful competitors toward group activities.

The inception into a nearby youth group is portrayed by a feeling of expectation and energy. For some, it is the primary openness to coordinated instructional courses, group elements, and the trained methodology that recognizes serious play. The progress from sporting play to organized preparing addresses a change in mentality, as youthful competitors figure out how to explore the complexities of cooperation, system, and the subtleties of their game under the direction of mentors and guides.

One of the essential parts of joining a nearby youth group is the development of a feeling of having a place and kinship. The group turns into a subsequent family, a companion of similar people limited by a shared objective. The common encounters, triumphs, and even mishaps manufacture bonds that reach out past the battleground. This feeling of local area turns into a wellspring of inspiration, offering close to home help during testing times and celebrating aggregate victories. The kinship inside youth groups contributes not exclusively to the competitors' athletic turn of events yet in addition to their self-improvement, encouraging characteristics of collaboration, correspondence, and versatility.

Organized instructional courses inside neighborhood youth groups acquaint youthful competitors with a routine that goes past the relaxed play of experience growing up. Mentors become coaches, directing competitors through expertise improvement, strategic comprehension, and functional preparation. The discipline imparted in these instructional meetings establishes the groundwork for a deep rooted enthusiasm for difficult work, devotion, and the quest for greatness. The change from individual abilities to group strategies highlights the significance of coordinated effort, correspondence, and key reasoning - abilities that stretch out past the limits of sports into different aspects of life.

The cutthroat idea of nearby youth groups adds a layer of fervor and challenge to the excursion. The excitement of wearing a group pullover, addressing one's local area, and contending with peers from different groups ingrains a feeling of obligation and pride. The serious climate turns into a proving ground for the abilities and methodologies mastered in preparing, furnishing youthful competitors with the valuable chance to apply their insight in a genuine setting. The encounters acquired from cutthroat play add to the improvement of versatility, flexibility, and a sound comprehension of progress and disappointment.

For the overwhelming majority youthful competitors, the choice to join a nearby youth group isn't just about playing a game; it is tied in with supporting a fantasy. Neighborhood groups frequently go about as venturing stones, giving a pathway to gifted people to progress in their wearing professions. The openness acquired through serious associations, competitions, and exploring open doors can open ways to more elevated levels of play, including school groups, local contests, and, surprisingly, public portrayal. Joining a neighborhood youth group, thusly, turns into an essential choice for those with desires of seeking after sports at further developed levels.

The impact of neighborhood youth groups reaches out past the improvement of athletic abilities. The group climate turns into a microcosm of society, where youthful competitors learn urgent life illustrations. The elements of cooperation show the significance of joint effort, correspondence, and shared regard. Competitors figure out how to explore assorted characters, oversee clashes, and value the qualities each colleague brings to the aggregate exertion. These relational abilities are instrumental with regards to sports as well as add to the general social and close to home improvement of youthful people.

Besides, neighborhood youth groups assume a huge part in cultivating a feeling of discipline and using time productively. Adjusting scholastics, instructional meetings, and cutthroat matches requires youthful competitors to foster authoritative abilities and focus on their responsibilities. The interest for predictable participation at instructional courses and adherence to group plans ingrains a feeling of obligation and responsibility. These examples in discipline become important resources that youthful competitors convey into their scholastic interests and future expert undertakings.

The excursion inside nearby youth groups isn't without its portion of difficulties. The tension of rivalry, the inescapable ups and downs, and the requests of offsetting sports with different parts of life can present critical obstacles. Notwithstanding, definitively these difficulties add to the improvement of flexibility and mental courage. Youthful competitors figure out how to adapt to difficulties, quickly return from routs, and comprehend that persistence is much of the time the way to long haul achievement. The experience of confronting difficulties inside a strong group climate turns into a developmental part of character improvement. The job of mentors inside neighborhood youth groups couldn't possibly be more significant. Mentors act as coaches, guides, and wellsprings of motivation for youthful competitors. Their mastery in the game, combined with their capacity to grant significant life illustrations, makes them instrumental figures in the improvement of yearning players. Mentors give specialized direction as well as sustain the profound and mental prosperity of their players. The mentorship given by mentors contributes fundamentally to the general development of youthful competitors, imparting in them an adoration for the game and a promise to constant improvement.

The effect of neighborhood youth groups on the more extensive local area is important. These groups frequently act as mobilizing focuses for networks, encouraging a deep satisfaction and solidarity. The help earned from families, companions, and nearby devotees makes a lively games culture that reaches out past the prompt players. The outcome of neighborhood youth groups turns into a wellspring of local area festivity, building up the possibility that sports have the ability to unite individuals and make a common feeling of character.

The inclusivity of neighborhood youth groups is one more prominent part of their effect. These groups frequently act as stages where people from different foundations meet up, separating hindrances of nationality, financial status, and social contrasts. The normal love for the game turns into a bringing together component that rises above individual contrasts, establishing a climate where variety is praised, and common regard is developed. The inclusivity inside neighborhood youth groups adds to the more extensive cultural story of sports as a power for social union and congruity.

All in all, joining nearby youth groups addresses an extraordinary excursion for youthful competitors, enveloping the improvement of athletic abilities as well as the development of fundamental abilities, versatility, and a feeling of local area. The choice to join a group is a cognizant decision to seek after an energy, embrace discipline, and be important for an option that could be bigger than oneself. The encounters acquired inside nearby youth groups reach out a long ways past the limits of sports, forming the person, values, and goals of youthful people.

As youthful competitors wear their group shirts and step onto the field, they leave on an excursion that impacts their own directions as well as adds to the dynamic embroidery of sports culture inside their networks. The tradition of nearby youth groups reverberations in the cheers of allies, the common recollections of triumphs and losses, and the persevering through influence on the existences of the people who hoped against hope and seek after their energy for the love of the game.

2. **Initial struggles and triumphs**

Beginning Battles and Wins: An Excursion of Versatility and Development

The excursion towards any critical objective is seldom a smooth direction; all things considered, it is many times set apart by a progression of starting battles that test one's purpose, strength, and assurance. These difficulties, however overwhelming from the beginning, act as cauldrons for individual and expert development, turning into the bedrock whereupon wins are fabricated. The story of introductory battles and wins is a general one, rising above social, topographical, and individual limits, winding around an embroidery of human experience that impacts anybody who has wandered into unfamiliar domains.

The commencement of any endeavor is loaded down with the fervor of conceivable outcomes, the adventure of fresh starts, and the expectation of progress. Notwithstanding, it is likewise a stage where the main murmurs of difficulties arise, frequently surprising people. The underlying battles go about as a reminder, requesting a recalibration of assumptions and a more profound comprehension of the responsibility expected to transform desires into the real world.

One of the ongoing ideas in the texture of beginning battles is the experience with the unexplored world. Whether setting out on another profession way, beginning a business, or chasing after an energy, the unfamiliar region presents a bunch of vulnerabilities. This vulnerability can be both elating and overwhelming, as people wrestle with inquiries regarding the reasonability of their objectives, the expected barriers ahead, and the penances required. Exploring the obscure requires strength, flexibility, and the ability to gain from each diversion.

Monetary limitations frequently arise as imposing beginning battles, especially for those wandering into business, seeking after advanced education, or beginning another endeavor. The beginning phases of an excursion are regularly set apart by restricted assets, expecting people to come to key conclusions about planning, asset designation, and monetary preparation. The experience of monetary requirements turns into a cauldron that tests genius, innovativeness, and the capacity to go with informed choices under tension.

The apprehension about disappointment poses a potential threat during the underlying phases of any undertaking. The strain to succeed, combined with the mindfulness that mishaps are an inborn piece of the excursion, can deaden. Conquering the feeling of dread toward disappointment is a critical achievement that frequently includes a psychological shift - seeing disappointments not as inconceivable obstructions but rather as venturing stones towards inevitable achievement. The capacity to embrace disappointment as an educator, extricating examples and experiences from mishaps, turns into a characterizing factor in the excursion of win.

The quest for greatness frequently includes a lofty expectation to learn and adapt, particularly in fields where dominance requires specific information and abilities. Securing skill requests persistence, devotion, and an eagerness to persevere through the underlying battles related with the growing experience. Whether it is dominating another dialect, procuring specialized abilities, or digging into the subtleties of a specific specialty, the underlying period of learning is a lowering encounter that lays the basis for future skill and certainty.

For those entering the expert domain, the test of showing what one can do in another climate is a typical subject. The working environment, with its extraordinary elements, assumptions, and progressive systems, can be a field where people face the underlying battles of laying out validity, tracking down their balance, and exploring workplace issues. Beating the obstacles of expert osmosis requires a mix of relational abilities, flexibility, and a guarantee to persistent improvement.

Enterprising endeavors frequently accompany a bunch of beginning battles that test the flexibility of visionaries and daring people. From tying down financing to building a client base, business visionaries explore a complicated scene where difficulties flourish. The capacity to endure the hardships of vulnerability, turn because of market criticism, and continue on through the unavoidable difficulties turns into a characterizing factor in the progress of enterprising undertakings.

The quest for imaginative undertakings, whether in human expression or development, isn't resistant to starting battles. Imaginative blocks, self-question, and the mission for creativity are difficulties that specialists, authors, and pioneers wrestle with at the start of their excursions. Win in the domain of imagination frequently rises out of the capacity to embrace weakness, push through imaginative blocks, and develop a mentality that considers difficulties to be valuable open doors for development.

In the domain of sports, competitors face the underlying battles of practical preparation, expertise refinement, and the tensions of rivalry. The excursion from fledgling to talented specialist includes exhausting preparation regimens, the discipline to defeat actual limits, and the psychological strength to push past one's apparent limits. Win in sports is frequently estimated by triumphs on the field as well as by the self-improvement that comes from overcoming starting battles.

The individual connections that structure an indispensable piece of human life likewise go through the cauldron of beginning battles. New kinships, heartfelt connections, and familial bonds are much of the time portrayed by a time of change, understanding, and discussion. The capacity to explore the intricacies of human associations, impart successfully, and develop sympathy becomes principal in building enduring and significant connections.

Nurturing, a significant excursion set apart by the introduction of a youngster, presents its own arrangement of introductory battles. Restless evenings, the lofty expectation to learn and adapt of providing care, and the changes expected to oblige another life test the flexibility and versatility of unseasoned parents. The victories in nurturing frequently lie in the little triumphs - the primary grins, the achievements accomplished, and the extending bonds produced through the difficulties.

The story of introductory battles and wins isn't just about beating outer difficulties yet additionally about going up against inward hindrances. Self-question, an inability to acknowledge success, and the internal pundit can be imposing enemies that people should explore on the way to progress. Win notwithstanding unseen conflicts includes developing mindfulness, rehearsing self-empathy, and cultivating an outlook of development and versatility.

The tales of famous figures across different areas frequently uncover the secret battles that went before their victories. From Thomas Edison's innumerable analyses prior to imagining the light to J.K. Rowling's dismissal letters before the progress of Harry Potter, these stories highlight the well known fact that wins are in many cases gone before by a progression of mishaps, difficulties, and snapshots of self-disclosure.

The groundbreaking idea of beginning battles lies in their ability to shape character, impart flexibility, and catalyze self-awareness. The excursion from battle to win is certainly not a straight movement however a repetitive course of getting the hang of, adjusting, and persisting. Wins, when seen from the perspective of beginning battles, become more than simple achievements; they become achievements in an excursion of self-revelation, strengthening, and the acknowledgment of one's true capacity.

The insight acquired from conquering introductory battles frequently turns into a wellspring of motivation for other people. The individuals who have endured storms, explored vulnerabilities, and arose victorious become encouraging signs and strength. Their accounts act as a demonstration of the groundbreaking force of diligence, the significance of embracing difficulties, and the innate limit inside each person to transform battles into wins.

All in all, the story of starting battles and wins is a demonstration of the versatility, persistence, and unyielding soul of the human experience. Whether chasing individual objectives, proficient greatness, or the supporting of connections, the excursion is set apart by difficulties that, when stood up to with boldness and assurance, make ready for win. The story of starting battles and wins is a common human story, a mosaic of encounters that mirrors the excellence of strength, the victory of the human soul, and the consistent pattern of development that characterizes the human excursion.

CHAPTER 3

Navigating the Challenges
Exploring the Difficulties: An Excursion of Versatility and Development

Life, with its multifaceted embroidery of encounters, presents a variety of difficulties that request route with flexibility, versatility, and an unflinching soul. The excursion of exploring difficulties is a widespread story that rises above social, topographical, and individual limits. It is a demonstration of the human limit with respect to development, the craft of conquering difficulty, and the groundbreaking power implanted during the time spent defying and overcoming snags.

The scene of difficulties is immense and various, going from individual battles to proficient obstacles, cultural issues, and worldwide emergencies. Each test, no matter what its tendency, conveys inside it the seeds of development and change. It is inside the cauldron of difficulty that people frequently find the profundity of their internal assets, strength, and the capacity to explore the intricacies of life.

The individual domain is frequently where people experience the most private and significant difficulties. Connections, both familial and heartfelt, can be a wellspring of delight and satisfaction but at the same time are fields where clashes, misconceptions, and close to home battles can emerge.

Exploring the difficulties inside private connections requires successful correspondence, compassion, and a readiness to comprehend and be perceived. The capacity to explore these complicated elements contributes not exclusively to the strength of individual associations yet additionally to the more extensive texture of social agreement.

Self-disclosure is an excursion that includes facing individual difficulties, whether they come from self-question, character emergencies, or the quest for legitimacy. The route of inner difficulties frequently requires thoughtfulness, mindfulness, and a guarantee to self-awareness. It is an excursion set apart by the investigation of one's qualities, convictions, and desires, as people endeavor to adjust their lives to their credible selves.

The expert domain presents its own arrangement of difficulties, from the beginning phases of vocation advancement to the intricacies of administration and authoritative elements. Exploring the difficulties of a profession includes consistent learning, variation to evolving scenes, and the capacity to conquer mishaps. The quest for greatness in one's expert undertakings frequently requests versatility even with disappointments, the ability to gain from botches, and the assurance to push through impediments.

Business venture, a way weighed down with vulnerabilities and dangers, is a demonstration of the craft of exploring difficulties. From tying down subsidizing to showcase variances and functional obstacles, business people continually wrestle with a horde of difficulties. The capacity to explore the tempestuous waters of business includes key reasoning, flexibility, and the fortitude to wander into the unexplored world. The narratives of fruitful business visionaries frequently reverberation with the examples gained from beating the unavoidable difficulties inborn in building and supporting a business.

The cultural scene is set apart by difficulties that request aggregate route. Issues like imbalance, separation, and social unfairness require purposeful endeavors to destroy fundamental boundaries and make a more evenhanded world. Exploring cultural difficulties includes promotion, compassion, and a promise to encouraging positive change. An excursion requires people and networks to face awkward insights, participate in troublesome discussions, and work cooperatively towards an all the more and comprehensive society.

Worldwide difficulties, for example, environmental change, pandemics, and international pressures, highlight the interconnectedness of the world. Exploring these mind boggling and extensive issues requires global collaboration, inventive arrangements, and a common obligation to the prosperity of the planet and its occupants. The capacity to explore worldwide difficulties requires a worldwide viewpoint, flexibility despite vulnerability, and an acknowledgment of the aggregate liability to shield what's to come.

Schooling, as a groundbreaking power, assumes a significant part in outfitting people with the abilities and information expected to explore the difficulties of the contemporary world. The quest for schooling includes conquering scholarly difficulties, embracing a development outlook, and developing a long lasting adoration for learning. The capacity to explore the difficulties inside the instructive excursion contributes not exclusively to self-awareness yet in addition to the more extensive headway of society.

The domain of wellbeing and prosperity is another field where people explore difficulties, from keeping a sound way of life to confronting clinical mishaps. The capacity to explore wellbeing challenges includes a comprehensive methodology that envelops physical, mental, and profound prosperity. It is an excursion set apart by taking care of oneself, versatility despite wellbeing mishaps, and the acknowledgment that prosperity is a dynamic and progressing process.

Nurturing, a significant excursion set apart by the obligation of sustaining and directing another life, presents its own arrangement of difficulties. From the restless evenings of outset to the intricacies of youthfulness, guardians explore a range of difficulties that require persistence, versatility, and unflinching affection. The capacity to explore the difficulties of nurturing includes a harmony between giving direction and permitting space to individual development, encouraging a steady climate, and embracing the delights and hardships of life as a parent.

The computerized age has introduced another arrangement of difficulties, from the intricacies of exploring on the web spaces to the effect of innovation on emotional well-being and cultural elements. Exploring the difficulties of the advanced period includes computerized proficiency, careful innovation use, and the capacity to adjust to the quickly developing scene of the virtual world. An excursion expects people to figure out some kind of harmony between the advantages and entanglements of innovation.

The most common way of exploring difficulties is definitely not a straight direction; a recurrent and dynamic excursion includes consistent variation and development. The capacity to explore difficulties is intently attached to the improvement of flexibility - the ability to quickly return from misfortunes, gain from encounters, and arise more grounded. Flexibility is certainly not a decent characteristic yet an expertise that can be developed through self-reflection, constancy, and a positive mentality.

The outlook with which people approach difficulties assumes an essential part in the route cycle. A development mentality, described by the conviction that capacities can be created through devotion and difficult work, engages people to consider difficulties to be open doors for learning and improvement. Developing a development mentality includes reexamining difficulties as brief snags and survey difficulties as venturing stones on the way to progress.

The capacity to appreciate people on a deeper level, the capacity to comprehend and deal with one's own feelings and explore the feelings of others, is one more fundamental expertise in the excursion of exploring difficulties. The capacity to understand people on a deeper level empowers people to answer difficulties with compassion, convey really, and fabricate positive connections. It includes mindfulness, self-guideline, social mindfulness, and relationship the executives.

The emotionally supportive networks that people develop assume a critical part in the route of difficulties. Whether through familial securities, kinships, mentorships, or local area associations, a powerful emotionally supportive network gives profound food, various points of view, and a feeling of having a place. Exploring difficulties turns into an aggregate exertion, as people draw strength from their encouraging groups of people and add to the development and versatility of others.

Versatility is a critical characteristic in the specialty of exploring difficulties. The capacity to adjust includes being available to change, embracing vulnerability, and changing systems because of developing conditions. In a world portrayed by fast changes, flexibility turns into a foundation in the route of difficulties, empowering people to flourish in unique and unusual conditions.

The account of exploring difficulties is deficient without recognizing the job of disappointment. Disappointment, a long way from being a last decision, is a necessary piece of the excursion. An instructor gives significant bits of knowledge, features regions for development, and cultivates modesty. The capacity to explore difficulties includes seeing disappointment not as a misfortune but rather as a venturing stone towards possible achievement.

The narratives of people who have explored critical difficulties frequently act as reference points of motivation. From verifiable figures who have molded the course of countries to ordinary legends who stand up to affliction with effortlessness, these stories highlight the flexibility implanted in the human soul. The capacity to change provokes into wins turns into a demonstration of the unstoppable will, innovativeness, and persistence that portray the human excursion.

All in all, exploring difficulties is a characteristic piece of the human experience, an excursion that includes the constant investigation of one's abilities, the development of strength, and the groundbreaking force of beating obstructions. Whether on an individual, proficient, cultural, or worldwide level, the route of difficulties is a unique cycle that requires a complex methodology. It is an excursion set apart by self-disclosure, development, and the acknowledgment that difficulties, when confronted with boldness and strength, become open doors for strengthening and change.

As people explore the intricacies of life, they contribute not exclusively to their self-awareness yet in addition to the aggregate development of mankind, winding around a story that praises the victory of the human soul even with difficulty.

3.1 Rising Through the Ranks

Ascending Through the Positions: An Excursion of Climb in Private and Expert Development

The climb through the positions, whether in the expert domain, self-awareness, or some other feature of life, is a convincing story that mirrors the natural human drive for progress, accomplishment, and self-acknowledgment. This excursion, set apart by a progression of steps and achievements, typifies the quest for greatness and the ceaseless mission for development. The story of ascending through the positions is a general one, resounding with people across different foundations, societies, and goals, as they explore the direction from commencement to dominance.

One of the essential areas where the idea of ascending through the positions is most clear is in the expert field. People frequently leave on their professions at passage level positions, overflowing with aspiration and a craving to have a significant effect. The excursion through the expert positions includes a course of ability improvement, experience gathering, and the showing of initiative characteristics. A trip requires diligence, commitment, and the capacity to adjust to the developing requests of the working environment.

At the start of an expert excursion, people commonly wind up in jobs where they are obtaining fundamental abilities and acquiring openness to the complexities of their picked field. This underlying stage is described by a lofty expectation to learn and adapt, as people retain information, refine their capabilities, and start to figure out the elements of their expert climate. Ascending through the positions in the expert domain includes dominating these basic components, fabricating a strong range of abilities, and laying out a standing for unwavering quality and capability.

As people progress in their professions, they frequently experience open doors for administration and administrative jobs. The climb through the positions requires specialized capability as well as the development of administration characteristics like successful correspondence, key reasoning, and the capacity to rouse and inspire others. Positions of authority carry with them new difficulties and obligations, denoting a critical progress in the excursion of expert development.

Mentorship and direction assume a significant part in the direction of ascending through the positions. Experienced tutors give bits of knowledge, share shrewdness, and deal support as people explore the intricacies of their vocations. Gaining from the individuals who have navigated comparative ways turns into an important resource, speeding up the course of development and offering a guide for progress. The coach mentee relationship is a cooperative one, adding to the improvement of the two players as they team up chasing greatness.

The excursion of ascending through the positions isn't without its portion of difficulties. People might confront snags like work environment elements, hierarchical changes, or times of expert vulnerability. Defeating these difficulties requires versatility, flexibility, and a development mentality. The capacity to see mishaps as any open doors for learning, to explore vagueness with certainty, and to persist notwithstanding difficulty turns into a sign of the people who effectively climb through the expert positions.

Business venture gives one more clear material to the story of ascending through the positions. Business visionaries frequently start with a thought, a dream that moves them into the difficult scene of business creation. The rising through the enterprising positions includes not just the improvement of a suitable plan of action yet additionally the capacity to explore vulnerabilities, secure financing, and adjust to showcase elements. Fruitful business people typify the soul of development, flexibility, and a tireless quest for their vision.

In the domain of self-improvement, the excursion of ascending through the positions is a groundbreaking investigation of self-disclosure and development. This excursion includes a guarantee to consistent learning, the development of new abilities, and the quest for interests and interests. Whether in the domains of wellbeing and health, imaginative pursuits, or scholarly undertakings, people climb through private positions by laying out and accomplishing objectives, defeating difficulties, and advancing into the best version of themselves.

The quest for instruction is a quintessential space where the story of ascending through the positions is profoundly imbued. Understudies set out on their scholastic processes determined to get information, improving decisive reasoning abilities, and procuring degrees that represent their scholarly climb. The move through instructive positions includes scholarly accomplishments, the investigation of different disciplines, and the improvement of a deep rooted love for learning. Graduating to higher scholarly levels addresses an unmistakable sign of the excursion's movement.

The account of ascending through the positions isn't restricted to formal instruction; it stretches out into the domain of individual interests and leisure activities. People who are enthusiastic about a specific discipline or work of art frequently end up climbing through the positions of capability and acknowledgment. Whether in sports, expressions, or some other pursuit, the excursion includes the commitment to consistent practice, refinement of abilities, and the quest for greatness that recognizes fledglings from specialists.

The idea of ascending through the positions is profoundly intertwined with the subject of initiative. Pioneers, whether in expert, local area, or individual settings, rise through the positions by typifying characteristics like vision, trustworthiness, and the capacity to motivate others. The excursion of initiative includes self-awareness as well as the strengthening and direction of the people who follow. Pioneers prepare for aggregate rising, establishing conditions where people can flourish and add to shared objectives.

Local area commitment and social effect give one more aspect to the account of ascending through the positions. Those focused on having a beneficial outcome in their networks rise through the positions of social impact by supporting causes, upholding for change, and effectively taking part in drives that add to everyone's benefit. The excursion includes cooperation, sympathy, and an unfaltering obligation to making positive cultural changes.

The rising through the positions is much of the time described by a change from individual accomplishment to aggregate effect. As people ascend through expert or individual positions, they progressively wind up in places where their impact stretches out past private accomplishment to the strengthening and advancement of others. The story develops from individual rising to a more extensive subject of commitment and mentorship, where the people who have climbed the positions become impetuses for the development of others.

The account of ascending through the positions is innately connected to the more extensive subject of versatility. The excursion includes confronting difficulties, defeating deterrents, and persevering chasing objectives. Strength isn't just about returning from disappointments yet additionally about getting the hang of, adjusting, and involving difficulties as venturing stones for additional climb. The capacity to explore difficulty with effortlessness and assurance is a principal quality of the individuals who effectively ascend through the positions.

With regards to ascending through the positions, the significance of equilibrium couldn't possibly be more significant. People should explore the requests of individual and expert development while keeping up with balance in different parts of their lives. Finding some kind of harmony among desire and prosperity, profession and individual life, and momentary objectives and long haul vision is critical for supported achievement and satisfaction all through the excursion.

The story of ascending through the positions is innately powerful and complex. It is an excursion set apart by nonstop development, where people navigate different progressive phases, gather encounters, and add to the development of others. The climb is definitely not a direct way however a nuanced investigation of conceivable outcomes, difficulties, and self-revelation. It is a demonstration of the human soul's ability for development, flexibility, and the quest for greatness in all spaces of life.

All in all, the story of ascending through the positions is a widespread excursion that epitomizes the human quest for progress, accomplishment, and self-acknowledgment. Whether in the expert domain, self-improvement, or cultural commitments, people set out on a powerful direction that includes ceaseless development, flexibility even with difficulties, and the strengthening of others. The rising through the positions is a significant investigation of human potential, an excursion that unfurls with each step, every achievement, and every commitment to the aggregate embroidery of individual and aggregate development.

1. **School and amateur leagues**
   School and Beginner Associations: Supporting Ability, Cultivating Energy, and Forming Prospects
   The harmonious connection among schools and beginner associations fills in as a foundation in the improvement of maturing competitors, encouraging an adoration for sports as well as supporting ability and molding

the future directions of people. The convergence of schooling and sports makes a powerful space where youthful competitors leave on an excursion of expertise improvement, collaboration, and self-awareness. This story investigates the significant effect of school and novice associations, enlightening their job in developing an enthusiasm for sports, imparting important fundamental abilities, and going about as pots for future athletic greatness.

Schools, as basic foundations of training, assume a critical part in acquainting youthful personalities with the universe of sports. Actual training programs structure a vital piece of the school educational plan, furnishing understudies with openness to different games, key abilities, and the significance of keeping a sound, dynamic way of life. The organized climate of school sports programs fills in as a ripe ground for ability ID and beginning expertise improvement.

Novice associations, then again, expand the excursion past the school entryways, offering a more extensive stage for youthful competitors to improve their abilities and take part in serious play. These associations, frequently coordinated at the local area or territorial level, give a scaffold between school sports and further developed degrees of rivalry. Novice associations go about as hatcheries for ability, setting out open doors for youthful competitors to exhibit their capacities, rival peers, and get acknowledgment for their commitment and ability in unambiguous games.

The collaboration among schools and beginner associations lies in the consistent progress from basic games projects to additional particular and cutthroat conditions. School sports lay the foundation by acquainting understudies with different games, permitting them to find their inclinations and aptitudes. As understudies progress, novice associations become roads for specialization, empowering them to zero in on unambiguous games and dive further into expertise advancement under the direction of devoted mentors and coaches.

Past the actual advantages of investment, school and novice associations contribute fundamentally to the all encompassing advancement of youthful people. Group activities, specifically, impart fundamental abilities like cooperation, correspondence, authority, and flexibility. The cooperative idea of group activities reflects true elements, getting ready understudies and youthful competitors for challenges they might experience in their future individual and expert lives.

With regards to school sports, the fellowship based on the battleground stretches out to the homeroom, making a positive and strong local area. Partners become something other than individual competitors; they become companions and partners, building up the possibility that achievement is an aggregate undertaking. The bonds produced during school sports programs frequently persevere past graduation, shaping an enduring organization of people who share a typical enthusiasm for sports and the qualities imparted through their athletic excursions.

Beginner associations, by their local area situated nature, cultivate a feeling of neighborhood pride and character. These associations frequently address explicit locales or neighborhoods, making a common feeling of having a place among members and allies. The people group commitment worked with by novice associations goes past the battleground, adding to the social texture and social character of the areas they address. The cheers from nearby observers, the help from loved ones, and the aggregate festival of triumphs become necessary components in the rich embroidery of local area sports.

The organized idea of school sports projects and beginner associations gives a fundamental scaffold to those seeking to seek after sports at more elevated levels. Gifted people recognized during their school years frequently track down a characteristic movement into additional cutthroat conditions, for example, school or college groups. The abilities and encounters collected in school and beginner associations become the establishment whereupon competitors can work as they progress to further developed degrees of rivalry.

Besides, the exploring systems implanted in beginner associations act as pipelines for distinguishing excellent ability. Scouts and mentors from more elevated level groups frequently successive beginner association matches to distinguish arising stars.

This cycle not just gives open doors to capable people to progress in their athletic interests yet additionally adds a layer of fervor and yearning to novice association contests. The fantasy about being explored and perceived for one's ability spurs youthful competitors to do everything they possibly can on the field, making a pattern of motivation and accomplishment.

The orientation inclusivity advanced by school and beginner associations contributes altogether to breaking orientation generalizations in sports. Customarily male-overwhelmed sports have seen a flood in female cooperation at the school and novice levels. The organized games programs in schools offer equivalent open doors for young men and young ladies to investigate and succeed in different games, testing cultural standards and cultivating a culture of orientation value. Novice associations, as well, frequently stress inclusivity, giving stages to female competitors to contend and grandstand their capacities on fair terms with their male partners.

While the cutthroat part of school and novice associations is unquestionable, the accentuation on sportsmanship, fair play, and character improvement stays a focal topic. Mentors and tutors in school sports projects and novice associations assume a vital part in imparting values like regard, trustworthiness, and discipline. The accentuation on moral lead and regard for rivals establishes a climate where competitors make progress toward triumph as well as perceive the significance of respect in both achievement and rout.

The effect of school and beginner associations isn't bound to the athletic domain; it reaches out to scholastic and self-improvement. Concentrates reliably feature the positive relationship between's sports support and scholastic accomplishment. The discipline, time usage abilities, and objective setting inborn in sports add to a balanced instructive encounter. The illustrations learned on the field - diligence, versatility, and the capacity to deal with pressure - emphatically affect an understudy's general scholastic presentation.

Besides, the openness to a cutthroat climate since early on imparts a mentality of ceaseless improvement and an eagerness to take on difficulties. Understudy competitors frequently figure out how to offset scholastic obligations with thorough preparation plans, leveling up their time usage abilities and hard working attitude. The capacity to shuffle scholastic and athletic responsibilities sets them up for the complex requests of grown-up life.

The idea of grants in view of athletic ability, frequently connected to accomplishments in school and beginner associations, opens ways to instructive open doors that might have been generally difficult to reach. Schools and colleges, perceiving the worth of understudy competitors, offer grants for the purpose of drawing in and supporting people who exhibit uncommon ability and obligation to their games. These grants become an acknowledgment of athletic accomplishment as well as a pathway to advanced education for the majority hopeful youthful competitors. The positive effect of school and beginner associations isn't restricted to the competitors alone; it reaches out to guardians, teachers, and the more extensive local area. Guardians assume a vital part in supporting and empowering their youngsters' cooperation in sports. The sidelines of school matches and novice association contests become spaces for families to meet up, cultivating a feeling of local area and shared excitement. The emotionally supportive network given by guardians, joined with the direction of mentors and educators, establishes an all encompassing climate for the development and improvement of youthful competitors.

Instructors perceive the significant effect of sports on generally speaking understudy improvement. The fundamental abilities developed on the battleground supplement the scholarly examples showed in homerooms. Thusly, schools frequently celebrate and incorporate games accomplishments into their more extensive instructive culture. The progress of school sports programs and the cooperation of understudies in beginner associations add to a lively and dynamic school soul.

All in all, the nexus among school and beginner associations frames a unique biological system that supports ability, cultivates energy, and shapes the fates of trying competitors. The excursion from school sports projects to novice associations addresses a continuum of development, learning, and improvement. The qualities imparted, the abilities sharpened, and the encounters acquired in this excursion reach out a long ways past the limits of the battleground, molding balanced people who convey the examples of sportsmanship, collaboration, and versatility into their future undertakings. As the world keeps on perceiving the significant effect of school and beginner associations, the story of athletic improvement stays a strong demonstration of the potential for positive change implanted in the combination of training and sports.

2. **Overcoming obstacles and setbacks**

Conquering Deterrents and Difficulties: The Tough Soul Even with Affliction

The excursion of life is loaded with difficulties, snags, and mishaps, framing a multifaceted woven artwork of encounters that characterize the human condition. It is inside the cauldron of difficulty that people are tried, their flexibility estimated, and their ability to defeat deterrents enlightened. This account investigates the significant topic of defeating obstructions and difficulties, revealing insight into the dauntless soul that arises even with misfortune and the groundbreaking influence implanted during the time spent transforming mishaps into venturing stones.

Obstructions, in different structures, manifest all through various features of life - individual, expert, scholastic, and then some. These boundaries can take the state of unforeseen disappointments, individual emergencies, outer limits, or the steady quest for aggressive objectives. How people explore and beat these obstructions turns into a demonstration of their personality, assurance, and capacity to change difficulties into potential open doors.

At the core of beating impediments lies the characteristic human nature of versatility. Strength isn't only returning from misfortune; it is the ability to adjust, learn, and fill notwithstanding difficulties. The account of flexibility is woven into the narratives of people who, in spite of confronting apparently unrealistic chances, transcend their conditions and arise more grounded, smarter, and more skilled than previously.

One of the essential components in defeating deterrents is the mentality with which difficulties are drawn closer. A development outlook, as instituted by clinician Song Dweck, is portrayed by the conviction that capacities can be created through devotion and difficult work. People with a development outlook see impediments as any open doors for learning and improvement instead of unrealistic barriers. This outlook shift turns into an incredible asset in exploring mishaps, as it energizes an emphasis on the most common way of beating difficulties as opposed to focusing on the actual impediments.

The excursion of defeating deterrents frequently starts with a significant affirmation of the circumstance within reach. It includes standing up to the truth of misfortunes, grasping the hidden causes, and embracing the close to home reactions that go with affliction. This period of thoughtfulness and acknowledgment is a urgent initial step, as it establishes the groundwork for versatility and the ensuing endeavors to overcome hindrances.

Individual mishaps, whether as wellbeing challenges, relationship emergencies, or existential dilemmas, frequently request a profound inner retribution. The capacity to go up against one's weaknesses, look for help from others, and develop self-empathy becomes vital. Beating individual mishaps is certainly not a single undertaking; it includes contacting others for direction, shaping an encouraging group of people, and perceiving the strength got from shared encounters.

In the expert domain, difficulties can appear as profession deterrents, project disappointments, or startling slumps. The story of conquering proficient mishaps is set apart by flexibility, key reasoning, and an eagerness to rethink objectives and approaches. People who explore proficient misfortunes actually frequently view difficulties as any open doors for development, reconsideration, and the development of abilities that add to future achievement.

Scholarly difficulties, whether as scholastic disappointments, learning incapacities, or instructive difficulties, request a strength that reaches out past the study hall. Conquering scholarly deterrents includes a guarantee to persistent getting the hang of, looking for elective ways to deal with schooling, and perceiving that knowledge isn't fixed however can be created through commitment and exertion. The tales of people who rise above scholastic misfortunes frequently feature the groundbreaking influence of persistence and an energy for information.

The quest for aggressive objectives is habitually joined by hindrances that test the constraints of one's assurance. Whether in business, imaginative pursuits, or athletic undertakings, people taking a stab at greatness experience mishaps that require a mix of steadiness and versatility. Beating mishaps chasing aggressive objectives includes a readiness to repeat, develop, and persevere notwithstanding vulnerability. The story of the individuals who accomplish uncommon accomplishments frequently uncovers an example of conquering various difficulties along the way to progress.

Misfortunes in the domain of emotional well-being, like nervousness, sadness, or other mental difficulties, present an exceptional arrangement of hindrances that require a nuanced way to deal with surviving. The excursion toward mental prosperity includes self-reflection, looking for proficient help, and the development of survival techniques. Conquering psychological well-being mishaps frequently requires destroying cultural marks of shame encompassing psychological wellness, encouraging open discourse, and establishing conditions that focus on close to home prosperity.

The social and social scenes wherein people explore their lives additionally present obstructions that request aggregate endeavors to survive. Separation, imbalance, and foundational obstructions can be considerable difficulties that require support, local area commitment, and a promise to civil rights. Defeating cultural hindrances includes testing dug in standards, enhancing minimized voices, and encouraging comprehensive conditions that destroy obstructions to advance.

Notwithstanding difficulties, the significance of a powerful emotionally supportive network couldn't possibly be more significant. Whether included family, companions, tutors, or a more extensive local area, an encouraging group of people turns into a wellspring of solidarity, direction, and support. The story of conquering hindrances is frequently interwoven with accounts of people who draw on the aggregate insight and backing of their organizations, changing misfortunes into shared wins.

Gaining from mishaps includes separating important illustrations and bits of knowledge from the experience. Every hindrance turns into a chance for self-revelation, ability advancement, and self-awareness. The capacity to ponder difficulties with a mentality of interest and strength permits people to get importance from challenges, encouraging a consistent pattern of progress and flexibility.

The most common way of conquering hindrances is certainly not a straight direction; it includes progress, difficulties, and iterative endeavors. The representation of misfortunes as venturing stones stresses the groundbreaking idea of the excursion. Every obstruction, when drawn nearer with flexibility and a development mentality, turns into a stage for rise, pushing people higher than ever of figuring out, capacity, and achievement.

The account of beating hindrances crosses with accounts of famous figures across different spaces who have confronted difficulty and arisen victorious. From Thomas Edison's various bombed tests prior to creating the light to J.K. Rowling's dismissal letters before the progress of Harry Potter, these stories highlight the generally accepted fact that mishaps are an inborn piece of the excursion toward progress. The capacity to endure even with difficulty, to see misfortunes as transitory diversions instead of super durable barricades, turns into a main quality of the people who make a permanent imprint on their individual fields.

Social stories, writing, and workmanship frequently mirror the subject of beating deterrents as a general and immortal theme. Courageous stories, fantasies, and tales from different societies epitomize the prototype excursion of confronting difficulties, doing combating winged serpents, and arising triumphant. These stories reverberate across ages, filling in as analogies for the human experience and the immortal journey for win over difficulty.

All in all, the story of defeating deterrents is a demonstration of the flexibility, strength, and dauntless soul of the human condition. It is an excursion set apart by difficulties that request boldness, flexibility, and the steadfast conviction that mishaps are not the end but rather an extraordinary part in the continuous story of individual and aggregate development. The story of conquering obstructions is a festival of the human soul's ability to change difficulty into valuable open doors, misfortunes into venturing stones, and difficulties into impetuses for significant and persevering through change.

3.2 Mentorship and Guidance

Mentorship, a cooperative relationship established in direction, shrewdness, and shared regard, remains as a foundation in the scene of individual and expert turn of events. The significant effect of mentorship rises above ages and teaches, enlightening the ways of the individuals who look for information, insight, and a guide for progress.

This story dives into the mind boggling elements of mentorship and direction, investigating the extraordinary force of these connections in forming people, cultivating greatness, and adding to the texture of aggregate development.

At its embodiment, mentorship is a powerful trade between a tutor, commonly an accomplished and prepared individual, and a mentee, somebody looking for direction and knowledge on their excursion. This relationship is described by trust, open correspondence, and a common obligation to the turn of events and development of the mentee. The coach fills in as an aide, offering information as well as giving significant life illustrations, shrewdness, and a viewpoint molded by experience.

One of the fundamental parts of mentorship is the transmission of implied information - the unwritten, experiential bits of knowledge that frequently escape formal training. While formal training gives an organized establishment, mentorship supplements it by offering a nuanced comprehension of certifiable intricacies. Coaches, drawing from their own encounters, share useful bits of knowledge, accounts, and viewpoints that overcome any barrier among hypothesis and application. This exchange of implied information turns into a basic part in getting ready mentees for the complex difficulties they will experience in their own and proficient lives.

The tutor mentee relationship is definitely not a one-size-fits-all model; rather, a tailor made association develops in view of the novel necessities, goals, and characters of the people in question. Compelling tutors perceive the uniqueness of their mentees, fitting direction to suit their particular settings and objectives. This customized approach recognizes that each mentee is on a particular excursion, and the job of the tutor is to enlighten the way instead of direct the objective.

Direction in the domain of expert improvement is a conspicuous feature of mentorship. Arising experts frequently explore an intricate scene loaded with vulnerabilities, industry complexities, and the quest for vocation objectives. Coaches, drawing from their own proficient excursions, give bits of knowledge into vocation directions, industry patterns, and viable procedures for progression. The coach turns into an essential partner, offering counsel as well as working with the mentee's admittance to organizations, potential open doors, and a more extensive comprehension of the expert scene.

Innovative endeavors, with their inborn vulnerabilities and difficulties, especially benefit from the directing hand of mentorship. Prepared business people, having endured the hardships of business, offer important experiences into exploring the perplexing territory of new companies. From key decision-production to gamble with the executives and development, tutors in the pioneering circle assume a urgent part in forming the achievement directions of their mentees. The guide's capacity to give a consistent hand and offer the insight acquired from the two triumphs and disappointments turns into a key part in the enterprising excursion.

In the scholastic domain, mentorship takes on a diverse job. Workforce tutors guide understudies in their scholarly interests as well as in exploring the intricacies of exploration, profession decisions, and self-improvement. The tutor mentee relationship in scholarly world stretches out past conventional training, frequently changing into deep rooted associations that length different phases of the mentee's profession. The direction given by scholastic coaches turns into a compass, guiding mentees toward significant commitments to their fields and cultivating a culture of scholarly development.

Mentorship isn't bound to expert or scholastic spaces; it reaches out to self-awareness and self-disclosure. Life tutors, frequently emerging from familial or local area associations, offer direction on exploring life's complexities, going with moral choices, and building significant connections. These coaches become wellsprings of intelligence, assisting people adjust their qualities to their activities and explore the ethical compass of their own excursions.

The mentorship story crosses with the subject of variety and consideration. Viable mentorship rehearses add to separating obstructions and establishing more comprehensive conditions. Coaches, by advocating variety, guide people from underrepresented bunches as well as effectively work to destroy fundamental predispositions inside their authoritative reaches. The tutor's job in cultivating inclusivity stretches out past direction; it includes support, setting out open doors, and engaging mentees to conquer hindrances established in orientation, race, identity, or different components of variety.

Switch mentorship, an idea acquiring unmistakable quality, challenges customary orders by perceiving that mentorship is a complementary trade of information. More youthful or less experienced people bring new viewpoints, innovative clever, and contemporary bits of knowledge that can help their more experienced tutors. This bidirectional progression of shrewdness and direction makes a powerful collaboration that mirrors the developing idea of mentorship in a quickly impacting world.

The groundbreaking force of mentorship is apparent in the accounts of people who have scaled extraordinary levels with the direction of tutors. From famous business pioneers to commended craftsmen and Nobel laureates, the consistent idea in numerous achievement stories is the presence of tutors who gave specialized direction as well as everyday encouragement and a confidence in the mentee's true capacity. These accounts highlight the significant effect of mentorship in forming the directions of unprecedented people.

Vital to the mentorship dynamic is the development of delicate abilities - relational abilities, correspondence, compassion, and the capacity to understand people on a deeper level. Viable coaches have specialized aptitude as well as succeed in these delicate abilities, establishing a climate where trust can prosper.

The guide's capacity to identify, tune in, and comprehend the novel difficulties looked by their mentees lays out the establishment for a relationship based on common regard and shared development.

The coach mentee relationship isn't resistant to challenges. The elements of force, correspondence styles, and varying assumptions can present intricacies that require cautious route. Tutors, perceiving the significance of cultivating a comprehensive and open climate, effectively look for input, adjust their methodologies, and make spaces where mentees feel engaged to communicate their necessities and desires. The tutor's capacity to be adaptable and receptive to the developing elements of the relationship is urgent in guaranteeing its viability.

Innovation, with its worldwide reach and interconnectedness, has reimagined the scene of mentorship. Virtual mentorship stages, online networks, and advanced specialized apparatuses have extended the opportunities for mentorship past topographical requirements. This computerized development, while improving availability, likewise presents new difficulties, for example, keeping up with the unique interaction and credibility that are necessary to successful mentorship.

The mentorship account reaches out to mentorship projects and drives that intend to organize the advantages of direction and backing. Corporate mentorship programs, for example, work with organized connections between experienced experts and arising ability inside associations. These projects contribute not exclusively to individual turn of events yet additionally to a culture of information sharing, joint effort, and consistent advancing inside the hierarchical setting.

Instructive establishments perceive the significant job of mentorship in understudy achievement and have carried out mentorship projects to help understudies' scholar and self-improvement. Peer mentorship drives, where more experienced understudies guide their friends, make a feeling of local area and backing inside scholastic conditions. These projects add to a positive learning society, cultivating a feeling of having a place and diminishing the feeling of detachment frequently experienced by understudies.

The mentorship story is deficient without recognizing the tutor's job in sustaining mentees' flexibility notwithstanding mishaps. Viable guides give a guide to progress as well as experiences into exploring disappointments and gaining from difficulties. The coach's own encounters of defeating difficulties become important stories that motivate flexibility and tirelessness in the mentee's excursion.

1. **Coaches and influential figures**
   Mentors and Powerful Figures: Shaping Lives, Developing Greatness, and Motivating Change
   The job of mentors and powerful figures in the embroidered artwork of human advancement rises above the bounds of sports fields or expert spaces. Whether on the battleground, in instructive settings, or inside the more extensive range of authority, these figures stand as signals of motivation, impetuses for change, and designers of greatness. This story investigates the multi-layered effect of mentors and persuasive figures, digging into the significant ways they profoundly mold lives, encourage individual and expert development, and rouse enduring change.

   At the center of training and mentorship is the craft of direction — a purposeful and frequently extraordinary interaction where experienced people share their bits of knowledge, information, and insight with those looking for course. Mentors, recognized by their capacity to lead, educate, and move, assume a vital part in the improvement of people across different spaces. While the games field is an unmistakable stage for instructing, the standards stretch out a long ways past, including instructive organizations, work environments, and local area settings.

   In the domain of sports, mentors possess a focal situation in the existences of competitors, filling in as engineers of both expertise improvement and character development. The effect of a mentor reaches out past the strategies and methodologies of the game; it pervades the actual texture of a competitor's character. Mentors, through their mentorship, impart values like discipline, collaboration, versatility, and a steady quest for greatness. The connection between a mentor and a competitor is frequently much the same as a harmonious organization, where the mentor's direction impels the competitor to more noteworthy levels, and the competitor's commitment turns into a demonstration of the mentor's impact.

The groundbreaking force of mentors is apparent in the stories of unbelievable games figures. From Phil Jackson, prestigious for his administration in b-ball, to Vince Lombardi, a famous figure in football training, these people made unrivaled progress on the field as well as made a permanent imprint on the existences of their players. The insight conferred by these mentors rises above the details of sports; it turns into an outline for initiative, strength, and the quest for greatness that reaches out a long ways past the battleground.

Instructive foundations are fruitful ground for compelling figures who act as mentors in the more extensive sense — teachers who guide understudies in scholarly pursuits as well as in the excursion of individual and character improvement.

These figures, frequently as educators, teachers, or coaches, assume a significant part in forming understudies' ways of living. The impact of a motivating instructor stretches out past the homeroom, pervading the decisions, values, and desires of their understudies.

In the expert domain, training takes on a key and initiative situated aspect. Chiefs, supervisors, and pioneers, frequently filling in as mentors to their groups, assume an essential part in encouraging a culture of joint effort, development, and constant improvement. The standards of training in an expert setting include ability improvement as well as the development of a development mentality, flexibility, and an aggregate feeling of direction. Powerful figures in administrative roles become engineers of hierarchical societies that focus on mentorship, learning, and the advancement of individual and aggregate potential.

Local area pioneers, activists, and powerful people of note act as mentors in the more extensive cultural setting, directing networks toward positive change, value, and civil rights. The extraordinary effect of these figures lies in their capacity to rouse aggregate activity, challenge foundational disparities, and encourage conditions where people can flourish regardless of their experiences. Their impact reaches out past way of talking; it turns into an impetus for grassroots developments, strategy changes, and the making of comprehensive spaces that mirror the upsides of equity and equity.

The story of instructing and mentorship crosses with the subject of variety and consideration. Viable mentors and powerful figures effectively work to destroy fundamental predispositions, champion variety, and establish conditions where people from all foundations feel esteemed and upheld. Their job becomes about direction and expertise improvement as well as about separating boundaries, enhancing minimized voices, and making pathways for underrepresented gatherings to succeed.

The idea of instructing likewise embraces the possibility of self-training — the interior discourse and self-direction that people utilize to explore difficulties, decide, and develop strength. In this sense, powerful figures stretch out past outside coaches to incorporate the horde voices, encounters, and methods of reasoning that people incorporate as they explore their own and proficient excursions. The tales of persuasive figures, whether as authentic symbols, contemporary good examples, or fictitious people, become directing lights that shape people's qualities, goals, and reactions to misfortune.

The impact of mentors and persuasive figures isn't bound to explicit jobs or titles; it reaches out to the regular collaborations and connections that shape the human experience. Guardians, companions, and tutors in different circles of life assume parts that encapsulate the standards of training. The insight shared during casual discussions, the help presented during testing times, and the consolation to seek after dreams all add to the mosaic of impacts that shape people's excursions.

The extraordinary force of training is established in the standards of sympathy, undivided attention, and a real obligation to the development and prosperity of others. Mentors and compelling figures who succeed in these characteristics establish conditions where people feel seen, heard, and esteemed. The capacity to interface on a human level, comprehend the one of a kind difficulties looked by others, and furnish direction with realness and care turns into the sign of successful instructing.

With regards to instructing and mentorship, the story likewise incorporates the idea of converse mentorship — a bidirectional trade of information and bits of knowledge. More youthful or less experienced people bring new points of view, innovative astute, and contemporary bits of knowledge that can help their more experienced partners. This proportional relationship challenges conventional orders and encourages a climate of nonstop learning and advancement.

The account of training and powerful figures converges with the topic of versatility. Powerful training includes the improvement of abilities as well as the development of a versatile mentality. Mentors and persuasive figures guide people in exploring misfortunes, gaining from disappointments, and fostering the psychological courage to persevere notwithstanding difficulties. The narratives of people who have conquered misfortune with the backing of tutors highlight the groundbreaking effect of strength developed through instructing connections.

Innovation, with its worldwide reach and interconnectedness, has re-imagined the scene of training and mentorship. Virtual instructing stages, online networks, and advanced specialized devices have extended the opportunities for mentorship past geological requirements. This advanced development, while improving availability, likewise presents new difficulties, for example, keeping up with the special interaction and genuineness that are indispensable to powerful training.

Training and powerful figures contribute not exclusively to individual turn of events yet in addition to the formation of societies and conditions that focus on development, learning, and greatness. Associations that embrace a training society, where pioneers effectively participate in mentorship and direction, frequently witness more significant levels of representative commitment, development, and generally achievement. The impact of instructing swells through groups, divisions, and whole associations, molding their aggregate character and direction.

All in all, the story of mentors and compelling figures is a significant investigation of the extraordinary effect that direction, shrewdness, and mentorship have on the human excursion. From sports fields to home-rooms, from meeting rooms to local area spaces, these figures impact lives, encourage greatness, and motivate getting through change. The story is a festival of the getting through power implanted in human associations, the insight shared across ages, and the dauntless soul of development and change that training and mentorship typify.

2. **Lessons learned on and off the field**

Illustrations Learned on and off the Field: The Crossing point of Sports and Life Shrewdness

The battleground, a microcosm of life's difficulties and wins, fills in as a significant study hall where people gather examples that reach out a long ways past the limits of sports. The equals between athletic undertakings and the excursion of life are rich with astuteness, offering experiences into strength, cooperation, administration, and self-awareness. This story digs into the illustrations learned on and off the field, investigating the extraordinary power implanted in the convergence of sports and life.

On the field, the excursion is accentuated by the back and forth movement of triumphs and losses, repeating the mood of life itself. The experience of rivalry trains people to explore the range of feelings — the delight of progress and the mistake of disappointment. These profound illustrations become impetuses for self-awareness, cultivating strength and an ability to defy difficulties with beauty and assurance.

The idea of cooperation, a foundation in sports, rises above its athletic starting points to turn into a similitude for cooperative progress in different features of life. Competitors gain proficiency with the significance of common help, correspondence, and shared objectives. The battleground turns into a material where people paint a representation of aggregate exertion, understanding that the strength of the group is more noteworthy than the amount of its singular parts. The illustrations of cooperation become adaptable abilities, affecting the elements of working environments, networks, and individual connections.

Initiative, exemplified by commanders and mentors on the field, turns into a core value for exploring life's difficulties. Competitors discover that powerful pioneers move, spur, and show others how its done. The skipper's job reaches out past scoring objectives or making plays; it includes imparting a feeling of direction, making a culture of responsibility, and cultivating a climate where each colleague feels esteemed. The authority illustrations learned on the field become diagrams for outcome in proficient undertakings and local area drives.

The idea of discipline, innate in the meticulousness of sports preparing, turns into a foundation for outcome in any space. Competitors gain proficiency with the worth of steady exertion, devotion, and the quest for greatness. The discipline developed on the field turns into an outlook that pervades scholastic pursuits, proficient obligations, and individual objectives. The capacity to lay out boundaries, stick to schedules, and endure despite difficulties turns into a sign of people who have guzzled the illustrations of discipline through sports.

In the cauldron of rivalry, competitors stand up to the truth of misfortunes and disappointments. These encounters, a long way from being simple losses, become venturing stones for development. Competitors discover that flexibility isn't tied in with keeping away from disappointments however about quickly returning, gaining from errors, and involving mishaps as impetuses for development. The field turns into a proving ground for the proverb that genuine strength lies not in staying away from falls yet in the capacity to ascend after each stagger.

The idea of sportsmanship, embodied in fair play, regard for rivals, and lowliness in triumph or rout, turns into a core value for exploring the intricacies of life. Competitors discover that honesty and moral direct are pretty much as significant as ability and procedure. The examples of sportsmanship stretch out past the battleground, affecting the person and moral compass of people as they participate in the more extensive range of human communications.

The dynamic of objective setting, major in sports, turns into an incredible asset for individual and expert achievement. Competitors figure out the significance of setting clear, quantifiable goals and working efficiently toward their accomplishment. The objective setting outlook, sharpened on the field, turns into a directing power for people as they explore scholarly pursuits, vocation directions, and the quest for individual yearnings.

The battleground turns into a material for variety and consideration, testing generalizations and cultivating a feeling of having a place regardless of foundations or contrasts. In the soul of rivalry, people figure out how to celebrate variety, perceiving that the strength of a group lies in its different sythesis. The examples of consideration become incredible assets for people as they participate in work environments, networks, and social drives.

Off the field, the examples of sportsmanship and fair play make an interpretation of into a promise to civil rights and value. Competitors, perceiving their impact, become advocates for inclusivity and problem solvers in tending to cultural disparities. The battleground turns into a take off platform for people who, furnished with the standards of reasonableness and equity learned in sports, add to making a more evenhanded world.

The illustrations of sportsmanship, strength, and cooperation find reverberation in the stories of notable competitors whose effect reaches out past the bounds of sports. Figures like Muhammad Ali, who exemplified mental fortitude and flexibility both all through the ring, become guides of motivation. These competitors, through their accounts of win and adversity, become living demonstrations of the getting through force of the examples learned on the field.

Mentors, tutors, and compelling figures in sports become life savers for competitors, giving specialized direction as well as bestowing life shrewdness. The connections manufactured with these compelling figures become wellsprings of motivation, forming the person and directions of people. The mentorship dynamic, intrinsic in sports training, turns into a model for direction and backing in different circles of life.

The battleground fills in as a stage for people to defy dread, test their cut-off points, and find the profundities of their capacities. Competitors discover that the quest for greatness requires pushing limits, embracing difficulties, and wandering past the safe place. The boldness developed on the field turns into a directing power for people as they explore individual and expert undertakings that request flexibility and dauntlessness.

The battleground turns into a microcosm of society, reflecting the two its assets and its imperfections. Competitors, through their encounters, become advocates for positive change, testing standards, and utilizing their impact to resolve social issues. The illustrations learned on the field become a source of inspiration, motivating competitors to utilize their foundation to add to the improvement of society.

The crossing point of sports and life insight is exemplified by the idea of "competitor mindset" — a mentality portrayed by discipline, tirelessness, and a persevering quest for objectives. Competitors, through their encounters on the field, foster mental determination, strength, and a development outlook that become priceless resources in exploring life's intricacies. The competitor mindset turns into a layout for people looking to defeat difficulties and make individual and expert progress.

In the story of examples learned on and off the field, the idea of equilibrium arises as a core value. Competitors figure out the significance of offsetting thorough preparation with rest, contest with fellowship, and individual accomplishment with aggregate achievement. The illustrations of equilibrium become fundamental apparatuses for people looking for amicability in their own and proficient lives.

The account of examples learned on and off the field highlights the getting through effect of sports on the human experience. Whether on the excellent phase of global contests or in neighborhood local area fields, the illustrations gathered from athletic undertakings become strings in the complicated embroidered artwork of individual and aggregate development. The battleground, as an illustration forever, turns into a material where people paint accounts of versatility, cooperation, initiative, and the getting through quest for greatness. In the orchestra of illustrations learned on and off the field, the reverberations of sportsmanship, discipline, and the unyielding human soul resound, making a story that rises above the limits of time and culture.

CHAPTER 4

The Crucible of Competition
The Pot of Rivalry: Manufacturing Character, Rousing Greatness, and Exploring Difficulties

The field of contest, a cauldron where people are tried, formed, and changed, remains as a microcosm of life's difficulties and wins. Whether on the games field, in scholarly pursuits, or inside the expert domain, the cauldron of contest turns into a material where character is manufactured, greatness is motivated, and people figure out how to explore the intricacies of progress and disappointment. This story digs into the multi-layered elements of the cauldron of contest, investigating its groundbreaking power in molding people, encouraging versatility, and filling in as an impetus for individual and aggregate development.

At its center, contest is a unique power that impels people to take a stab at progress, test their cutoff points, and seek after greatness. The battleground, whether it be an arena, a homeroom, or a meeting room, turns into a phase where people defy difficulties, exhibit their abilities, and take a stab at triumph. The cauldron of contest, with its intrinsic pressure, turns into a strong impetus for self-revelation, pushing people to investigate the profundities of their true capacity.

In the domain of sports, the pot of contest turns into a characterizing component in the stories of competitors. From the adrenaline-filled snapshots of triumph to the piercing encounters of rout, competitors explore a range of feelings inside the pot of contest. The games field, with its power and unconventionality, turns into a proving ground for strength, sportsmanship, and the capacity to perform under tension. Competitors discover that the cauldron of contest isn't just about winning or losing; it is about the excursion, the illustrations learned, and the person produced chasing greatness.

The idea of sportsmanship, characteristic for the cauldron of contest, rises above the scoreboard. Competitors discover that genuine triumph includes capable play as well as regard for adversaries, trustworthiness, and modesty in progress or rout. The pot of rivalry turns into a study hall where people retain the standards of fair play, fellowship, and the comprehension that the quintessence of contest lies in the common quest for greatness as opposed to simple victory over others.

Past games, the cauldron of rivalry appears in scholastic pursuits, where understudies fight with the difficulties of assessments, undertakings, and scholarly thoroughness. The scholastic field turns into a cauldron where people develop discipline, decisive reasoning, and an enthusiasm for information. The opposition for scholarly greatness, set apart by steadiness and scholarly interest, turns into an extraordinary excursion that reaches out past the homeroom, molding the directions of deep rooted students.

In the expert domain, the cauldron of rivalry characterizes the scene of professions, organizations, and businesses. Experts explore the difficulties of a serious market, where development, versatility, and vital insight become fundamental credits. The cauldron of rivalry in the expert field encourages a culture of nonstop improvement, pushing people and associations to develop, enhance, and remain ahead in a dynamic and consistently evolving scene.

The pot of rivalry additionally meets with the topic of authority. Pioneers, whether in sports, the scholarly community, or business, are produced in the cauldron of contest. The capacity to rouse groups, settle on essential choices under tension, and explore the intricacies of contest turns into a sign of viable initiative. Pioneers discover that the pot of rivalry isn't just about individual accomplishments yet in addition about establishing conditions where aggregate greatness can flourish.

The illustration of the cauldron highlights the extraordinary force of difficulty inside the serious field. Difficulties, disappointments, and startling difficulties become the cauldron where people face their weaknesses, refine their techniques, and arise more grounded. The pot of rivalry helps people to see obstructions not as unconquerable boundaries but rather as any open doors for development and learning. The strength developed notwithstanding difficulty turns into an important resource that people convey into all parts of life.

The pot of contest, while encouraging individual development, likewise sustains a feeling of aggregate personality and having a place. Groups, whether in sports or cooperative workplaces, explore the pot of contest together. The common quest for shared objectives, the fellowship manufactured in the cauldron, and the shared help during difficulties become characterizing components of a group's excursion. The pot of rivalry turns into a space where people learn not exclusively to succeed separately yet in addition to add to the outcome of a more prominent group.

The idea of fair contest turns into a foundation inside the pot, underlining the significance of moral lead, uprightness, and adherence to rules. In the cauldron of fair rivalry, people discover that achievement accomplished through unscrupulousness or unjustifiable practices is empty and misses the mark on getting through fulfillment that comes from certifiable accomplishment. The cauldron turns into a space where character is tried, and people arise with a feeling of trustworthiness that directs their activities both inside and past the serious field.

The cauldron of contest isn't bound to the physical or proficient areas; it additionally penetrates the social and cultural texture. Countries, in the cauldron of worldwide rivalry, fight for financial matchless quality, mechanical progressions, and international impact. The standards of fair play, regard for variety, and coordinated effort become fundamental in exploring the intricacies of global relations. The pot of rivalry at the worldwide level highlights the interconnectedness of countries and the common difficulties that request aggregate arrangements.

The accounts of notable figures frequently mirror the extraordinary excursions inside the pot of rivalry. From competitors who ascend from lack of clarity to guarantee Olympic gold to business people who explore the difficulties of the business world, these accounts resound with the general subject of defying difficulties, pushing limits, and making progress inside the cauldron of contest. The stories of these figures become wellsprings of motivation, representing that the pot isn't simply a proving ground yet in addition a stage for remarkable accomplishments.

The pot of contest likewise interlaces with the subject of individual personality. People find aspects of themselves inside the pot, revealing qualities, shortcomings, and inert possibilities. The pot turns into a mirror reflecting not just the outer markers of progress or disappointment yet in addition the inward excursion of self-revelation and development. The examples advanced inside the pot add to the forming of a powerful and versatile individual personality.

The cauldron of rivalry, while cultivating greatness, additionally brings up issues about the expected entanglements of hyper-intensity. The strain to continually outflank, the feeling of dread toward disappointment, and the constant quest for progress can prompt burnout, tension, and a slanted identity worth. It becomes basic to adjust the drive for greatness with an acknowledgment of the significance of prosperity, emotional well-being, and the inherent worth of the excursion inside the pot.

Innovation, with its quick progressions and worldwide availability, acquaints new aspects with the pot of rivalry. Advanced stages, virtual fields, and online commercial centers rethink the idea of contest, making it more available yet additionally more perplexing. The computerized pot highlights the requirement for versatility, advanced proficiency, and a nuanced comprehension of the developing elements inside the cutthroat scene.

In the instructive domain, the pot of rivalry brings up issues about the adequacy of frameworks that put unreasonable accentuation on grades, rankings, and state sanctioned testing. The quest for scholarly greatness inside a serious structure frequently requires a reexamination of instructive ideal models, zeroing in on individual accomplishments as well as on cultivating imagination, decisive reasoning, and an affection for learning. The cauldron turns into a space where instructors and policymakers wrestle with the sensitive harmony between cultivating sound contest and supporting comprehensive development.

All in all, the cauldron of rivalry arises as a strong power that shapes people, characterizes societies, and drives social orders forward. Whether on the games field, in scholarly pursuits, or inside the expert field, the pot turns into a groundbreaking space where character is tried, flexibility is fashioned, and greatness is propelled. The stories inside the cauldron resound with widespread topics of win, difficulty, and the persevering through human soul. In the orchestra of rivalry, the pot turns into a dynamic and developing creation, mirroring the heap manners by which people explore difficulties, fashion characters, and add to the aggregate embroidery of human experience.

4.1 College and National Tournaments

School and Public Competitions: The Landmarks of Desire, Kinship, and Wearing Magnificence

School and public competitions stand as meaningful milestones where dreams come to fruition, ability is sharpened, and the soul of contest flourishes. These fields, whether on the university stage or the public stage, become cauldrons that shape the accounts of competitors, fashion enduring recollections, and raise the embodiment of donning greatness. This investigation digs into the multi-layered elements of school and public competitions, unwinding the strings of yearning, fellowship, and the quest for wearing magnificence that characterize these essential contests.

The University Stage: A Platform for Dreams

School competitions, throbbing with young extravagance and the commitment of potential, act as a platform for trying competitors.

These contests, whether in ball, football, soccer, or heap different games, become fields where people change from the crudeness of secondary school sports to the organized power of university rivalry. The university stage is where gifts are distinguished, supported, and frequently, shot onto the public and worldwide scenes.

The appeal of school competitions lies chasing triumph as well as in the fellowship manufactured inside groups. Competitors, frequently entering school as outsiders, structure bonds that rise above the battleground. The common triumphs, routs, and the aggregate quest for greatness become the groundwork of kinships that endure forever. The brotherhood inside school groups turns into a microcosm of the bigger donning local area, encouraging a feeling of having a place and mutual perspective.

For some competitors, school competitions address the zenith of long stretches of commitment and difficult work. The possibility of wearing the shades of one's school and contending at a more elevated level turns into a wellspring of monstrous pride. School competitions grandstand the variety of ability across colleges, establishing a climate where competitors push limits, exhibit their abilities, and test their determination against impressive adversaries. The enthusiasm and energy of school competitions add to the lively embroidered artwork of university games, injecting grounds with an irresistible soul of rivalry.

Past the adventure of contest, school competitions offer competitors a priceless stage for individual and athletic turn of events. The organized preparation regimens, direction from experienced mentors, and openness to more elevated levels of play add to the all encompassing development of people. Competitors refine their specialized abilities as well as develop characteristics like discipline, collaboration, and flexibility - credits that reach out a long ways past the battleground.

School competitions are not restricted to the spotlight of well known sports; they likewise envelop a different cluster of disciplines, including discussion, chess, and different esports. These competitions become mixtures of ability, cultivating a culture where understudies from various scholarly disciplines unite to feature their abilities and seek after greatness in their picked spaces. The inclusivity of school competitions reflects the variety of school life itself, giving open doors for people changed interests and gifts to sparkle.

The story of school competitions stretches out past the games field to incorporate the social and social texture of grounds. Competitions become events for festivity, encouraging a feeling of local area and pride. The energetic environment during school competitions, with fans wearing group tones and mobilizing behind their competitors, makes an electric climate that rises above the limits of the battleground. The comprehensive developments, exhibitions, and the tangible feeling of school soul add to the energetic woven artwork of school life.

Public Competitions: The Zenith of Wearing Goal

Public competitions, remaining as the pinnacle of wearing goal, hoist contest to a terrific stage where the most elite join to strive for incomparability. These competitions, whether as public titles, Olympic preliminaries, or other zenith occasions, address the perfection of long stretches of commitment, preparing, and penance. The way to public competitions is frequently cleared with provincial contests, qualifying adjusts, and a steady quest for greatness.

The meaning of public competitions stretches out past individual greatness; it turns into an issue of public pride. Competitors contending on the public stage convey the expectations and goals of their nation, exemplifying the aggregate soul of a country. Public competitions become cauldrons that produce public characters, where people contend for individual accomplishment as well as to carry distinction to their country.

The serious scene of public competitions is described by its power and the combination of first class ability. Competitors who have succeeded at provincial and university levels presently face the best in the country, establishing a climate where the edges of triumph are razor-slight, and each presentation is examined on the most excellent scale. The strain of public competitions is both a pot and an impetus, pushing competitors to arrive at new levels of accomplishment.

The excursion to public competitions is frequently weighed down with accounts of flexibility, assurance, and the capacity to conquer difficulty. Competitors explore the afflictions of preparing, face considerable adversaries, and defy the psychological and actual difficulties inborn in arriving at the public stage. The stories that unfurl inside public competitions become stories of win despite everything, adding layers of motivation to the more extensive account of wearing greatness.

Public competitions likewise act as grandstands for arising ability, giving a stage to youthful competitors to influence the public scene. The possibility of contending with laid out stars turns into a catalyzing force for rising gifts, prodding them to feature their abilities and report their appearance on the excellent stage. Public competitions subsequently become milestones for experienced competitors as well as theaters where new stars arise and shape the eventual fate of their individual games.

The social meaning of public competitions stretches out to the fan base, making an aggregate encounter that resounds the nation over. Fans rally behind their public groups, shaping an ocean of varieties and serenades that resonate through arenas and fields. The common feelings, the ups and downs of every rivalry, become strings in the woven artwork of public personality. Public competitions join different networks under a typical flag, encouraging a feeling of having a place and pride in shared accomplishments.

The tradition of public competitions is frequently interlaced with notable minutes and unbelievable competitors who scratch their names into the chronicles of wearing history. These competitions become the stage for records to be broken, noteworthy contentions to unfurl, and the unyielding human soul to be on full showcase. Snapshots of win and tragedy inside public competitions become carved in the aggregate memory, representing the getting through force of sports to charm and rouse.

Public competitions additionally add to the worldwide account of sportsmanship and global kinship. Contending countries meet up in the soul of fair play, common regard, and a common love for the game. The connections between competitors from various countries, the trading of social subtleties, and the festival of variety become basic parts of the more extensive account that unfurls inside the field of public competitions.

The effect of public competitions reaches out past the quick rush of triumph or the failure of rout. These competitions become impetuses for grassroots turn of events, rousing the up and coming age of competitors desire for significance. The perceivability and glory related with public competitions add to the development of sports at the grassroots level, making a pipeline of ability that guarantees the progression of greatness in the wearing scene.

All in all, school and public competitions stand as cauldrons where the fantasies of competitors come to fruition, where the soul of contest flourishes, and where the quest for greatness turns into an aggregate undertaking. These milestones, whether on school grounds or public fields, become microcosms of human yearning, strength, and the getting through quest for brandishing magnificence. The stories that unfurl inside these competitions weave an embroidery that rises above the limits of time and culture, epitomizing the immortal soul of contest and the widespread journey for significance.

1. **Intense rivalries and defining moments**
   Extraordinary Competitions and Pivotal occasions: The Substance of Donning Show
   In the rich woven artwork of sports, extraordinary competitions and vital turning points arise as the strings that wind around together the story of athletic ability, energy, and the dauntless human soul. These components lift games past simple contests; they change games into epic shows that dazzle hearts, rise above borders, and become scratched in the aggregate memory of fans. This investigation dives into the quintessence of extraordinary contentions and extremely important occasions, disentangling the elements that make them integral to the appeal of sports.
   Extraordinary Contentions: The Heartbeat of Brandishing Show
   Serious contentions are the thumping heart of sports, mixing contests with a profound intensity that rises above the limits of the battleground. Whether it's the noteworthy conflicts between Genuine Madrid and Barcelona in soccer, the immortal fights between the Boston Red Sox and the New York Yankees in baseball, or the savage matchups between Serena Williams and Maria Sharapova in tennis, contentions add a layer of force that lifts the stakes and changes each experience into a scene.
   The pith of serious competitions lies chasing triumph as well as in the well established history, social importance, and the instinctive energy that fans offer of real value. Contentions frequently have verifiable predecessors, with conflicts going back many years, in the event that not hundreds of years, making a story bend that stretches out past individual matchups. The social and provincial components of extreme contentions

add to the feeling of personality and having a place that fans partner with their groups, lifting each experience to a fight for matchless quality and pride.

The development to a competition match is in many cases joined by uplifted feelings, intense expectation, and a substantial feeling of show. It rises above the Xs and operating system of the game, digging into the domains of custom, heritage, and the heaviness of assumptions. Players, mindful of the verifiable importance, play for themselves as well as for the traditions of the people who wore the shirt before them. The power of the contention turns into a pot where players are produced, where snapshots of brightness or errors can become deified in the legend of the game.

Serious contentions additionally act as cauldrons for sportsmanship, testing the limits of cutthroat soul and shared regard. While the on-field fights might be wild, off the field, competitors frequently recognize the common quest for significance, perceiving the job their adversaries play in pushing them higher than ever. These snapshots of shared regard, whether in post-match handshakes or slow time of year communications, become fundamental parts of the mind boggling embroidered artwork that is woven inside the elements of extreme competitions.

The effect of serious contentions reaches out past the players and groups included; it resonates through the fan base, making networks that focus intensely on with the fortunes of their #1 groups. The extreme feelings that go with competition matches act as a binding together power, uniting fans in a common encounter that rises above the limits of language, culture, and foundation. Competition matches become common occasions where the result shapes the aggregate state of mind, and the boasting freedoms acquired or lost wait in the air until the following standoff.

The life span of extreme competitions, traversing ages and ages, adds an immortal quality to sports. These competitions become piece of the social legacy, went down through families, turning into a common inheritance that interfaces people across time. The accounts of famous matches, unbelievable rebounds, and severe losses become the oral practices that tight spot fans, players, and networks in a tough bond.

Vital crossroads: The Woven artwork of Athletic Heritage

Vital crossroads in sports are the brushstrokes that paint the material of athletic heritage. There the direction of a game, a season, or even a lifelong turns on the support of brightness, strength, or sheer dauntlessness. Whether it's Michael Jordan's notorious "Influenza Game" in ball, Usain Bolt's record-breaking runs in olympic style events, or the Wonder on Ice in hockey, vital turning points take shape the substance of brandishing show.

What recognizes pivotal occasions isn't simply the excellent expertise shown however the unique circumstance, the stakes, and the account bend paving the way to that solitary case. These minutes become the permanent depictions that typify the soul of rivalry, the victory over difficulty, or the acknowledgment of athletic potential pushed as far as possible. Extremely important occasions rise above the limits of the actual game; they become social standards, images of motivation, and benchmarks against which future accomplishments are estimated.

In the cauldron of vital turning points, competitors frequently become modelers of their own heritage. These minutes are not just glimmers of splendor; they are the climax of long stretches of commitment, preparing, and a tireless quest for greatness. The long periods of training, the penances made, and the flexibility developed notwithstanding mishaps unite in the particular case that carves a competitor's name into the archives of donning history.

The effect of extremely important occasions stretches out past individual competitors to the groups, urban communities, and countries they address. These minutes become shared encounters that join fans in an aggregate story of win and greatness. The Marvel on Ice, where the longshot U.S. hockey group crushed the stalwart Soviet Association at the 1980 Olympics, goes past the actual game; it encapsulates the victory of coarseness, assurance, and the faith in the unprecedented. Such pivotal occasions become piece of a city or country's personality, filling in as a wellspring of pride and motivation for ages.

The expectation paving the way to vital crossroads, the vulnerability of the result, and the close to home delivery that follows add to the show that characterizes sports. The stories that unfurl inside these minutes frequently make no sense, prearranging stories of flexibility that reverberate generally. These minutes become shared social recollections, where fans clearly review where they were and the way that they felt while seeing a competitor hold onto significance in the cauldron of rivalry.

Vital crossroads additionally act as microcosms of the human experience, exemplifying subjects of determination, fortitude, and the capacity to conquer unrealistic chances. Competitors who adapt to the situation at these times become images of human potential, moving people to stand up to difficulties in their own lives with a comparative soul of assurance. The effect of pivotal occasions reaches out past the bounds of the battleground, becoming signals that guide people in their own and proficient undertakings.

While the spotlight frequently radiates on individual heroics in pivotal turning points, the job of cooperation and aggregate exertion can't be put into words. Many pivotal occasions are the consequence of consistent coordination, trust among colleagues, and a common obligation to a shared objective. Whether it's a somewhat late objective in soccer or a signal blender in ball, these minutes frequently include the cooperative energy of a group working as a firm unit.

In the domain of group activities, pivotal occasions become the achievements that shape the character of an establishment or a public group. The Chicago Bulls' predominance during the 1990s, accentuated by Michael Jordan's down winning shots, characterizes a period in ball. Essentially, the New Britain Nationalists' rebound in Super Bowl LI against the Atlanta Birds of prey turns into a part in the celebrated history of the establishment. These vital turning points add to the tradition of groups, making stories that resound with fans and become piece of the social legacy of the game.

Taking everything into account, extreme contentions and vital turning points arise as the twin support points that maintain the greatness of sports. The show inside serious contentions, with its close to home intensity and authentic reverberation, lifts rivalries to exhibitions that rise above the limits of the battleground. Pivotal occasions, then again, become the glowing sparkles that enlighten the story of athletic heritage, epitomizing the substance of versatility, brightness, and the quest for significance. Together, these components structure the spirit blending ensemble that resounds through the fields, arenas, and fields, enthralling the hearts of fans and deifying sports as a demonstration of the unprecedented potential outcomes innate in the human soul.

2. **Emerging as a standout player**

Arising as a Champion Player: The Excursion of Ability, Persistence, and Change

The way to arising as a champion player in the realm of sports is a nuanced venture set apart by ability disclosure, persevering steadiness, and groundbreaking development. From the grassroots levels to the zenith of expert contest, competitors go through a course of development that stretches out past actual ability to envelop mental flexibility, versatility, and the capacity to explore the intricacies of the donning scene.

This investigation digs into the multi-layered elements of arising as a champion player, disentangling the strings that wind around together the story of athletic climb.

At the beginning of each champion player's process lies the disclosure of natural ability. Whether it's a youthful footballer exhibiting excellent ball control, a tennis wonder showing a characteristic fondness for accuracy, or a b-ball player with an inborn feeling of court mindfulness, ability fills in as the natural substance that separates people. The beginning phases of ability disclosure frequently happen at the grassroots level, where mentors, tutors, and even individual players perceive and sustain the uncommon capacities that recognize a sprouting competitor.

The supporting of ability includes specialized expertise improvement as well as the development of an energy for the game. Champion players frequently show an inherent love for their game, a certifiable happiness got from the demonstration of playing. This energy turns into the main impetus that impels people to contribute incalculable hours sharpening their specialty, pushing limits, and looking for nonstop improvement. The combination of ability and enthusiasm turns into the establishment whereupon the excursion of arising as a champion player is fabricated.

As competitors progress through the formative stages, from youth associations to secondary school rivalries, they experience a horde of difficulties that request something beyond actual ability. The psychological part of the game becomes the dominant focal point, requiring flexibility, center, and the capacity to explore the inescapable misfortunes that intersperse the excursion. The champion player, in the pot of contest, figures out how to embrace disappointment as a venturing stone to progress, developing a mentality that perspectives challenges not as unconquerable impediments but rather as any open doors for development.

The progress from beginner to first class levels frequently includes openness to more elevated levels of contest, where champion players separate themselves through a mix of expertise, versatility, and the capacity to perform under tension. The champion player's process turns into a story of flexibility, as they stand up to new strategic intricacies, face rivals with different playing styles, and explore the increased assumptions that go with more elevated levels of contest. This flexibility, frequently alluded to as a player's "football level of intelligence," "court mindfulness," or "game sense," turns into a main trait that separates champion players.

Mentorship assumes an essential part in the excursion of arising as a champion player. Mentors, experienced players, and compelling figures become guides who refine specialized abilities as well as grant shrewdness on system, sportsmanship, and the elusive components that add to greatness. The guide understudy dynamic turns into a channel for the exchange of information, experience, and the qualities that shape the personality of champion players. Mentorship, at its center, is a relationship that rises above the specialized parts of the game, imparting a feeling of direction, discipline, and a guarantee to consistent improvement.

Champion players frequently end up at the convergence of chance and readiness. The cutting edge minutes, where ability takes shape into on-field splendor, are much of the time catalyzed by a juncture of elements - a key game, a critical presentation, or an unforeseen open door. Whether it's a youthful soccer player procuring a spot in the beginning setup, a ball prospect making a game-dominating shot, or a tennis player prevailing in a high-stakes match, these minutes become characterizing parts in the story of arising as a champion player.

The idea of champion players isn't bound to individual brightness; it additionally reaches out to the capacity to add to the progress of the group. The champion player, inside the group dynamic, turns into an impetus for aggregate greatness. They raise the exhibition of everyone around them, set out open doors for partners, and epitomize the standards of administration, collaboration, and magnanimity. The champion player's effect rises above measurements; it is appeared in the attachment, strength, and shared outcome of the group.

The development of champion players remains forever inseparable with a comprehensive comprehension of the game - a mindfulness that reaches out past individual execution to envelop the complexities of group procedure, resistance examination, and the more extensive elements of the game. The champion player develops into an understudy of the game, engrossing the specialized subtleties as well as the essential keenness that supports accomplishment at first class levels. This exhaustive comprehension turns into a competitive edge, enhancing the effect of their actual ability with a cerebral way to deal with the game.

The excursion of arising as a champion player isn't without its portion of penances. The obligation to preparing systems, the discipline to stick to dietary plans, and the penances made as far as private time and relaxation exercises become basic parts of the champion player's way of life. The quest for greatness requests a comprehensive methodology that incorporates actual wellness, mental prosperity, and a way of life lined up with the requests of significant level rivalry.

Champion players frequently end up push into the spotlight, becoming competitors as well as individuals of note and diplomats for their game. The capacity to deal with the tensions of popularity, to carefully maintain effortlessness in triumph and lowliness in disgrace, turns into an expansion of the champion player's personality. The impact they employ, both on and off the field, conveys an obligation to move the future, add to the development of the game, and act as good examples for trying competitors.

The excursion of arising as a champion player isn't direct; it is interspersed by pinnacles and valleys, triumphs and mishaps. Wounds, variances in structure, and the rhythmic movements of the serious scene add to a story of flexibility and the capacity to return quickly from difficulty. The champion player's process is a demonstration of the human ability to endure, adjust, and fill despite difficulties.

4.2 National Team Call-Up

Public Group Call-Up: The Zenith of Athletic Accomplishment and Public Pride

A public group call-up is the peak of a competitor's excursion, addressing individual accomplishment as well as the zenith of public pride. It is an honor gave to a limited handful who have shown extraordinary expertise, commitment, and consistency in their separate games. This height to the public stage denotes a turning point in a competitor's profession, exemplifying individual accomplishment as well as the exemplification of a country's brandishing desires.

The call to address one's country is a climax of long stretches of difficult work, penance, and steadfast responsibility. Competitors who get the sought after public group call-up have navigated the complex pathways of grassroots turn of events, youth institutes, and expert associations. This excursion is set apart by endless long periods of preparing, refining abilities, and contending at different levels, each step adding to the competitor's development and availability for the public stage.

The meaning of a public group call-up reaches out past individual accomplishment; it is an impression of a competitor's effect on the wearing scene. Competitors who get this call are not only champion players; they are diplomats for their game, exemplifying the best expectations of expertise, sportsmanship, and commitment. The public group call-up is an acknowledgment of current ability as well as of the possibility to rouse and lead, both on and off the field.

For some competitors, the public group call-up is an acknowledgment of life as a youngster dreams. From kicking a ball in the neighborhood to scoring objectives in nearby associations, the excursion is permeated with the fantasy about wearing the public tones and addressing one's country. This call-up changes youth desires into an unmistakable reality, making a significant association between the competitor and the aggregate longs for a country.

The declaration of a public group call-up is a snapshot of significant importance, both for the competitor and their encouraging group of people. Families, mentors, partners, and fans share in the delight of this accomplishment, perceiving that the call-up isn't simply a singular victory however a common achievement. The overflow of help, salutary messages, and the feeling of common pride intensify the meaning of the public group call-up, changing it into a second that reverberates across networks.

The public group call-up is definitely not a single occasion; it is implanted in the more extensive story of public personality and pride. The competitor, by addressing the public group, turns into an image of the nation's wearing ability and a wellspring of motivation for the future. The call-up adds to the development of a donning society, encouraging excitement, and supporting the ability that will shape the fate of the country's athletic undertakings.

The excursion from neighborhood rivalries to the public group frequently includes openness to assorted playing styles, methodologies, and social subtleties. Competitors chose for public obligation wind up in a mixture of ability, encompassed by peers who have succeeded in different associations and rivalries. This conjunction of ranges of abilities turns into a cauldron for individual and aggregate development, as competitors figure out how to adjust, team up, and contribute their interesting assets to the public group.

The hit up to the public group carries with it a bunch of liabilities that rise above the limits of the battleground. Competitors become envoys for their game as well as for their country. Their activities, both on and off the field, are examined and celebrated as impressions of public person. The call-up is a challenge to maintain the upsides of sportsmanship, regard, and fair play, turning into a good example for hopeful competitors and a wellspring of pride for the whole country.

The groundwork for public group obligations includes thorough instructional courses, strategic meetings, and the digestion of a different gathering of competitors into a strong unit. Group science becomes vital as players, frequently addressing various clubs and associations, meet up to frame a brought together power. The capacity to manufacture securities, impart successfully, and comprehend the qualities of colleagues becomes as basic as individual abilities. The public group call-up isn't simply an affirmation of individual ability; it is an encouragement to add to the aggregate outcome of the group.

Public group contests, whether as mainland titles, World Cups, or Olympic Games, raise the stakes and power of rivalry. The public group call-up is a challenge to take part in these esteemed occasions, where competitors contend for individual magnificence as well as for the honor and pride of their country. The heaviness of addressing the expectations and assumptions for a nation adds a layer of tension that requires mental strength, flexibility, and the capacity to perform under the most splendid spotlight.

The effect of a public group call-up reaches out to the competitor's club, association, and the more extensive wearing biological system. Clubs invest heavily in supporting ability that rises to the public stage, exhibiting the adequacy of their improvement programs. Associations, by contributing players to public groups, build up their remaining as cauldrons of ability and seriousness. The progress of competitors at the public level turns into a demonstration of the energy and strength of the wearing designs inside a country.

The public group call-up is frequently joined by snapshots of reflection and appreciation. Competitors offer thanks to their mentors, guides, partners, and every one of the people who play had an impact in their excursion.

The call-up turns into a chance to recognize the aggregate exertion that has impelled the competitor to this crossroads. The lowliness shown during these snapshots of acknowledgment highlights the upsides of cooperation and mentorship that are fundamental to the competitor's turn of events.

1. **Representing the country**

    Addressing the country in the domain of sports is a significant honor and a zenith accomplishment for any competitor. It means individual accomplishment as well as the exemplification of a country's donning goals and pride. The excursion from nearby rivalries to the public stage is an extraordinary odyssey, set apart by devotion, expertise improvement, and steady responsibility. Competitors who procure the honor of addressing their nation have navigated a way that reaches out from grassroots improvement to proficient associations, with each step adding to their development and preparation for the difficulties of global contest.

    The meaning of addressing the nation lies in the singular achievement as well as in the more extensive setting of public character. Competitors decided to wear the public varieties become images of the nation's donning ability, conveying the expectations and assumptions for their kinsmen. This emblematic portrayal rises above the battleground, penetrating the social texture of the country and adding to the development of an aggregate feeling of satisfaction and character.

    The declaration of a competitor's choice to address the nation is a snapshot of significant importance. It is a demonstration of the competitor's expertise, difficult work, and consistency, however it is likewise a common achievement celebrated by families, mentors, partners, and fans. The call to address the nation is certainly not a singular accomplishment; a shared victory resounds across networks and builds up the interconnectedness between individual achievement and aggregate pride.

    The excursion towards addressing the nation commonly starts in the cauldron of neighborhood contests and youth associations. Competitors grandstand their abilities in these developmental stages, grabbing the eye of scouts, mentors, and tutors who perceive their true capacity. The sustaining of ability turns into a cooperative exertion including mentors who give direction, guides who offer insight, and colleagues who add to the competitor's improvement inside a strong environment.

    As competitors progress through the formative stages, the excursion turns out to be more nuanced, requesting an all encompassing way to deal with expertise improvement and mental backbone. The change from grassroots rivalries to proficient associations is in many cases set apart by expanded degrees of rivalry, strategic intricacies, and openness to different playing styles. Competitors figure out how to adjust, team up, and explore the complexities of the donning scene, setting them up for the difficulties that anticipate at the public level.

The call to address the nation isn't simply an acknowledgment of current ability; it is an affirmation of the competitor's capability to move and lead. Competitors who wear the public tones become representatives for their game, exemplifying the best expectations of ability, sportsmanship, and devotion. Their activities, both on and off the field, are investigated and celebrated as impressions of public person, adding a layer of liability to the honor of public portrayal.

For some competitors, the call to address the nation is the acknowledgment of experience growing up dreams. From kicking a ball in the neighborhood to scoring objectives in nearby associations, the excursion is saturated with the fantasy about wearing the public tones and remaining on the worldwide stage. This change from youth goals to a substantial reality makes a significant association between the competitor and the aggregate longs for a country.

The groundwork for addressing the nation includes something beyond actual preparation; it requires mental guts, versatility, and the capacity to work as a feature of a firm group. Competitors chose for public obligations wind up in instructional courses, strategic meetings, and agreeable matches that set them up for the afflictions of global contest. The science inside the group becomes fundamental as players, frequently addressing various clubs and associations, meet up to frame a brought together power.

Public group rivalries, whether as mainland titles, World Cups, or Olympic Games, raise the stakes and force of contest. The call to address the nation is an encouragement to take part in these esteemed occasions, where competitors contend for individual greatness as well as for the honor and pride of their country. The heaviness of addressing the expectations and assumptions for a nation adds a layer of tension that requires mental mettle, versatility, and the capacity to perform under the most brilliant spotlight.

The effect of addressing the nation reaches out past individual competitors to their clubs, associations, and the more extensive donning environment. Clubs invest wholeheartedly in sustaining ability that rises to the public stage, exhibiting the adequacy of their improvement programs. Associations, by contributing players to public groups, support their remaining as pots of ability and intensity. The outcome of competitors at the public level turns into a demonstration of the dynamic quality and strength of the brandishing structures inside a country.

The call to address the nation is frequently joined by snapshots of reflection and appreciation. Competitors express because of their mentors, coaches, partners, and every one of the people who play had an impact in their excursion. The call to address the nation turns into an amazing chance to recognize the aggregate exertion that has impelled the competitor to this crossroads. The lowliness shown during these snapshots of acknowledgment highlights the upsides of cooperation and mentorship that are indispensable to the competitor's turn of events.

The meaning of addressing the nation isn't restricted to the prompt wearing setting; it adds to the more extensive story of public personality and pride. Competitors become images of greatness, versatility, and the dauntless soul of the country. The accounts of their triumphs and battles become piece of the aggregate memory, adding layers to the social embroidered artwork of the country.

2. **Pressure, pride, and national glory**

The conversion of tension, pride, and the quest for public brilliance frames the pot in which competitors addressing their nation track down themselves. The excursion from grassroots advancement to the public stage is stamped by ability and commitment as well as by the heaviness of assumptions and the longing to carry distinction to one's country. This interaction of tension and pride makes a unique that shapes the competitor's outlook, impacts execution, and adds to the more extensive story of public personality.

Pressure, with regards to addressing the nation, is diverse. It radiates from the uplifted assumptions for fans, the heaviness of history and custom, and the familiarity with being a leading figure for the country. The eyes of the whole nation are on the competitor, and the greatness of this obligation can be both overwhelming and elating. Whether it's an extra shot in a football World Cup last, a vital serve in a Davis Cup match, or a definitive shot in an Olympic occasion, the strain to convey rises above the limits of the battleground.

The assumptions put on competitors addressing their nation are intensified by the energy and enthusiasm of fans. Public pride, imbued in the social texture, changes sports into an aggregate encounter where triumphs are commended as mutual victories, and losses are felt as shared dissatisfactions. The strain to live up to these aggregate assumptions can be an extra layer that competitors should explore, and the capacity to channel this tension into inspiration turns into an essential part of their psychological versatility.

However, pressure, when embraced and bridled, can be an impetus for significance. Competitors who flourish with the enormous stage frequently have a novel capacity to transform tension into fuel, involving the heaviness of assumptions as a wellspring of inspiration as opposed to a weight. The pot of tension turns into a produce where competitors are tried, and their reactions to crucial minutes can characterize individual vocations as well as add to the rich embroidery of wearing history.

Pride, then again, is the personal center that ties competitors to the demonstration of addressing their country. It is the profound feeling of association with one's underlying foundations, culture, and the aggregate history of the country. Pride isn't just a singular feeling however a common feeling that resounds across networks and ages. The pride in wearing the public tones is a sign of the penances, the difficult work, and the unfaltering responsibility that have characterized the competitor's excursion.

For competitors, addressing their nation is an honor that goes past private accomplishment. It is an honor to turn into an image of public greatness and a wellspring of motivation for trying competitors. The pride in addressing the nation is apparent not just in the competitor's presentation on the field yet additionally in their direct off it. The modesty showed, the affirmation of encouraging groups of people, and the appreciation communicated during snapshots of progress all mirror the's comprehension competitor might interpret the more extensive meaning of their job as a public delegate.

The quest for public magnificence, frequently acknowledged through triumphs in worldwide rivalries, turns into a definitive goal for competitors addressing their country. The potential chance to bring back a World Cup, an Olympic gold decoration, or a mainland title is the finish of long stretches of difficult work and a demonstration of the competitor's expertise, assurance, and strength. The quest for public greatness isn't just about private awards; it is tied in with drawing one's name into the records of the nation's brandishing history.

The mission for public magnificence is intrinsically interwoven with the more extensive account of public character. Fruitful public groups become images of versatility, solidarity, and the capacity to defeat difficulties. The accounts of notorious triumphs, emotional rebounds, and snapshots of individual splendor become piece of the aggregate memory, adding to the social legacy of the country. Public brilliance in sports turns into a wellspring of pride that stretches out past the battleground, penetrating different parts of society.

The strain to accomplish public greatness is a ceaseless propensity in the existences of competitors. A lot is on the line, and the edges among progress and frustration are many times razor-meager. The weight of assumptions can be constant, and the capacity to deal with this strain turns into a principal quality of competitors who climb to the culmination of their game. The quest for public brilliance isn't for the cowardly; it requires mental grit, versatility despite difficulties, and a tenacious obligation to greatness.

The elements of strain, pride, and the quest for public brilliance are generally tangible during significant worldwide competitions. Occasions like the FIFA World Cup, the Olympics, or local titles hoist the power of contest, making each match a public display. The intensity of fans, the media examination, and the information that the eyes of the world are watching add layers of intricacy to the competitor's insight. These competitions become cauldrons where the transaction of strain and pride arrives at its apex.

In these high-stakes rivalries, competitors frequently end up confronting minutes that characterize professions. A punishment shootout, a last-minute objective, or a near tie can become permanent pictures that resound through time.

The strain to act in these conclusive minutes is enormous, yet so too is the amazing chance to scratch one's name into the pantheon of public legends. The quest for public greatness expects competitors to endure this strain as well as to transcend it and convey when it makes the biggest difference.

The stories of competitors who prevail chasing public greatness frequently follow a recognizable curve. These are people who, in the cauldron of strain, track down supplies of flexibility and boldness. They are driven by private desire as well as by a firmly established obligation to the aggregate yearnings of their country. Their exhibitions become snapshots of therapy for a nation, joining different networks under a typical pennant of pride and festivity.

In any case, the quest for public brilliance isn't generally delegated with progress. Misfortunes and losses are innate in the eccentric idea of sports. Competitors, notwithstanding the heaviness of strain and the profundity of public pride, may end up on some unacceptable side of the outcome. These snapshots of frustration become similarly characterizing, testing the competitor's personality and versatility. The capacity to quickly return from rout, to gain and develop from difficulties, is a significant part of the excursion.

CHAPTER 5

Professional Ascent

The excursion of expert climb in the realm of sports is a nuanced investigation of ability, constancy, and the relentless quest for greatness. Competitors progressing from the beginner positions to the expert field explore a perplexing scene set apart by elevated contest, expanded assumptions, and the requests of a profession devoted to their picked sport. This climb isn't just a movement in expertise and actual ability; a comprehensive change envelops mental courage, versatility, and the capacity to explore the complexities of the expert wearing biological system.

The progress from crudeness to impressive skill is an essential point in a competitor's vocation. It addresses not just the finish of long stretches of committed preparing yet in addition the start of another section set apart by higher stakes and heightened examination. The choice to seek after an expert profession is many times joined by a significant obligation to the game, as competitors embrace the difficulties and potential open doors that accompany contending at the most elevated levels.

At the core of the expert rising is the competitor's ability, the undiscovered potential that separates them from their companions. Whether it's the artfulness of a footballer on the field, the accuracy of a golf player on the course, or the readiness of a tumbler in contest, natural ability turns into the establishment whereupon the expert excursion is fabricated. Mentors, scouts, and ability spotters assume a urgent part in distinguishing and sustaining this ability, perceiving the potential for outstanding execution at the expert level.

The supporting of ability reaches out past specialized expertise improvement to include a profound comprehension of the game's subtleties. Proficient competitors are not simply genuinely capable; they have an exhaustive comprehension of procedure, game elements, and the psychological versatility expected to perform under the most difficult conditions. The expert rising includes a consistent course of learning and refinement, as competitors drench themselves in the key and strategic components of their picked discipline.

Mentorship turns into a directing power in the expert climb. Mentors, prepared players, and compelling figures inside the wearing local area become significant wellsprings of intelligence and direction. The coach mentee relationship stretches out past specialized guidance to incorporate experiences into the mental parts of significant level contest, the craft of overseeing achievement and misfortunes, and the development of an outlook equipped towards supported greatness.

As competitors rise to the expert positions, they experience an increased degree of rivalry that fills in as both a cauldron for refinement and a litmus test for their capacities. Proficient associations, competitions, and rivalries become fields where ability is exhibited, and competitors should reliably show their value in the midst of a field of similarly talented companions. The expert climb is certainly not a direct direction; it includes adjusting to new playing styles, beating difficulties presented by rivals, and exploring the physical and mental afflictions of the expert circuit.

The psychological part of the game becomes the overwhelming focus in the expert field. Competitors should foster a strength that permits them to climate the tensions of assumption, manage the unavoidable mishaps, and keep up with center despite interruptions. The capacity to perform reliably at the most significant level requires a psychological backbone that supplements actual ability, and competitors frequently work with sports clinicians to sharpen this part of their game.

Actual wellness turns into a non-debatable part of the expert climb. The requests of expert contest require a degree of molding that goes past what is expected at the beginner level. Competitors stick to thorough preparation regimens, custom-made sustenance plans, and recuperation conventions to guarantee that their bodies can endure the power of expert play.

The quest for greatness turns into a day in and day out responsibility that reaches out to each feature of a competitor's way of life.

The expert climb is many times interspersed by crucial minutes that shape a competitor's profession. These minutes could be advancement exhibitions that declare their appearance on the expert stage, pivotal triumphs that lift their remaining in the game, or characterizing occasions where they show flexibility even with misfortune. These minutes act as markers in the story of expert rising, drawing the competitor's name in the aggregate memory of fans and companions.

As competitors progress in their expert vocations, they become representatives for their game. Their exhibitions on the worldwide stage add to the prevalence and development of the game, drawing in new fans and rousing the up and coming age of competitors. The expert rising isn't just a singular excursion; it is a commitment to the more extensive biological system of the game, forming its direction and impacting its social importance.

The way of life of an expert competitor includes the excitement of contest as well as the obligations that accompany being an individual of note. Competitors become brands no matter what anyone else might think, and their lead on and off the field adds to their picture and heritage. Drawing in with fans, taking part in local area drives, and taking care of media commitments become vital parts of the expert climb, adding layers of intricacy to the competitor's everyday existence.

Wounds, a lasting test in the realm of sports, can fundamentally influence the direction of the expert rising. Competitors should fight with the actual cost of their picked sport, go through restoration processes, and frequently face the vulnerability of recuperation timetables. Conquering wounds requires actual restoration as well as mental versatility, as competitors explore the personal difficulties of mishaps and work towards recovering their pinnacle structure.

The expert climb isn't absent any trace of the business side of sports. Competitors participate in dealings with clubs, patrons, and the executives, and grasping the elements of agreements, supports, and brand organizations turns into a fundamental expertise. Monetary education becomes vital as competitors deal with their income, speculations, and long haul monetary preparation. The expert climb includes succeeding on the field as well as exploring the intricacies of the games business.

The worldwide idea of pro athletics implies that competitors frequently end up addressing a group as well as their country on the global stage. Public group call-ups and support in worldwide contests become basic parts of the expert climb. The potential chance to contend at the most elevated level, wearing the public tones, adds a layer of renown to the competitor's excursion and adds to their inheritance inside the more extensive setting of the game.

The expert rising is a powerful excursion that develops as time passes. Competitors should stay versatile, constantly refining their abilities, and embracing new systems to remain ahead in a cutthroat scene. The development of an expert competitor includes a harmony among experience and the long for ceaseless improvement, a fragile balance that characterizes supported accomplishment at the most significant levels.

5.1 Club Debut

The club debut in the realm of sports is an original second that denotes the change from wannabe to member in the expert field. For competitors, this inception into the cutthroat scene of expert clubs is a climax of long stretches of devotion, difficult work, and expertise improvement. The presentation is a transitional experience, an emblematic section into the echelons of expert play, and a second that reverberates with the singular competitor as well as with fans, mentors, and partners put resources into the progress of the club.

At the center of the club debut is the competitor's excursion through formative stages, from grassroots levels to youth foundations and frequently through the positions of hold or junior groups associated with the expert club. These stages act as cauldrons for ability recognizable proof and expertise improvement, permitting mentors and headhunters to evaluate the competitor's true capacity and availability for the afflictions of expert play.

The presentation is many times gone before by a time of expectation and readiness. Competitors go through thorough preparation regimens, strategic meetings, and mental molding to guarantee they are exceptional for the requests of expert rivalry. Mentors assume an essential part in this planning, offering direction on system, giving bits of knowledge into the subtleties of the game at the expert level, and imparting a mentality helpful for progress on the field.

The meaning of the club debut reaches out past individual accomplishment; it is a common second celebrated by the competitor's encouraging group of people, including family, companions, and coaches who play had an impact in the formative excursion. The presentation turns into an impression of aggregate endeavors, a demonstration of the competitor's responsibility, and an affirmation of the help got from the people who have supported their ability.

For fans, the club debut is a snapshot of fervor and interest. It is the presentation of another player into the crew, a chance to observe the abilities and potential that stand out. The expectation encompassing an introduction can add a component of strain, however it likewise adds to the feeling of event and the profound reverberation existing apart from everything else.

The elements of a club debut differ across sports. In football (soccer), a presentation might include the player entering the field as a substitute or procuring a spot in the beginning setup. In cricket, it very well may be the main appearance in an expert match, with the player taking to the pitch to bat, bowl, or field. No matter what the game, the introduction is a door to the expert positions, a stage into the spotlight, and an opportunity to demonstrate one's courage on the large stage.

The profound range encompassing a club debut is huge. For the competitor, it is a mix of fervor, anxiety, and a significant feeling of achievement. Venturing onto the field wearing the club tones is an acknowledgment of a fantasy supported since the beginning of playing the game. It is an affirmation that long periods of commitment and determination have prompted this second, and the presentation turns into an individual achievement carved in the competitor's excursion.

The serious idea of elite athletics implies that a presentation isn't just a stately event; it is a trial of the competitor's capacities under the investigation of fans, mentors, and rivals. The debutant must consistently coordinate into the group dynamic, comprehend and execute strategic plans, and exhibit the abilities that procured them the open door in any case. The introduction turns into a microcosm of the competitor's true capacity, offering a brief look into what they bring to the group.

In group activities, the science between players is urgent, and the debutant should rapidly adapt to the correspondence and playing styles of their colleagues. The capacity to fashion associations on the field, grasp the implicit subtleties of group elements, and contribute definitively to the aggregate exertion is a sign of an effective introduction. Mentors distinctly see how the debutant supplements the group's system and adjusts to the speed and power of expert play.

The club debut isn't generally an account of moment achievement. Competitors might confront difficulties, experience misfortunes, or wrestle with the tensions related with playing at the expert level. It is entirely expected for debutants to encounter a scope of feelings, from the euphoria of a top notch play to the dissatisfaction of mix-ups or botched open doors. The capacity to explore these variances, keep calm, and gain from the experience becomes indispensable to the competitor's development.

The effect of a club debut reaches out to the more extensive story of the group and the club. An effective presentation can infuse a feeling of positive thinking and energy into the crew, electrifying colleagues and imparting trust in the training staff. On the other hand, a difficult introduction can act as a learning an open door, inciting a time of reflection and change in accordance with guarantee future achievement. The presentation, regardless of the prompt result, adds to the group's aggregate process and adds layers to the advancing story of the club.

For mentors and the executives, the presentation is a snapshot of approval for ability ID and player improvement programs. It means that the competitor has advanced through the formative positions, satisfied the guidelines set by the instructing staff, and is considered prepared for the difficulties of expert contest. The outcome of a debutant ponders emphatically the club's obligation to sustaining ability and putting resources into what's to come.

The post-debut stage includes a consistent course of transformation and improvement. Competitors dissect their presentation, get criticism from mentors, and participate in designated preparing to address explicit areas of advancement. The presentation turns into a springboard for additional development, spurring the competitor to refine their abilities, improve how they might interpret the game, and contribute without fail to the group's prosperity.

The club debut is much of the time the first of a large number in a competitor's expert profession. Resulting appearances, accomplishments, and commitments to the group's prosperity add layers to the story, forming the competitor's heritage inside the club. The introduction fills in as a primary section, and the competitor's process unfurls with each resulting match, making an embroidery of encounters, victories, and difficulties.

The close to home reverberation of a club debut stretches out to fans, whose association with the group is frequently entwined with the stories of individual players. Debutants become heroes in the aggregate story of the club, and fans put genuinely in their excursions. The help and consolation from fans can be a wellspring of motivation for debutants, cultivating a feeling of having a place and a common desire for progress.

1. **Joining a professional team**

   Joining an expert group in the realm of sports is a groundbreaking encounter that denotes the climax of long stretches of difficult work, devotion, and expertise improvement. For competitors, this change from crudeness to incredible skill addresses a huge achievement — an approval of their ability and a section into a cutthroat field where the stakes are higher, and the assumptions are enhanced. The excursion to joining an expert group is a complex interaction, including ability distinguishing proof, discussions, variation to another climate, and the reconciliation into the group dynamic.

   The way to joining an expert group frequently starts in the pot of formative associations, youth foundations, or university rivalries. Here, competitors grandstand their abilities, grab the eye of scouts, and become piece of the ability pool that expert groups effectively screen. Scouts assume a critical part in ability distinguishing proof, scouring nearby, public, and, surprisingly, worldwide contests to recognize players with the possibility to have an effect at the expert level.

   The enrollment cycle is a fragile dance, with scouts and ability spotters intently assessing a competitor's specialized capacities as well as their psychological mettle, flexibility, and potential for development. The choice to welcome a player to join an expert group is in many cases in light of a complete evaluation of their general reasonableness for the requests of expert rivalry. Exchanges then, at that point, follow, including conversations on agreements, terms of commitment, and the job the competitor is supposed to play inside the group.

   The second a competitor gets a proposal to join an expert group is one of significant importance. It is an approval of their ability, a demonstration of their persistent effort, and a confirmation of their likely in the serious scene. This proposition is many times joined by a blend of energy, expectation, and a feeling of obligation as the competitor considers the excursion ahead. The choice to join an expert group isn't simply a lifelong move; a life changing decision impacts a competitor's direction in the realm of sports.

   The progress from the formative stage to an expert group includes not just an adjustment of the degree of rivalry yet additionally a change in outlook and assumptions. Competitors should adjust to the expanded power, examination, and amazing skill that describe the highest levels of their game. The transition to an expert group connotes a move forward in expertise prerequisites as well as a submersion into the complexities of the expert wearing biological system.

The combination into an expert group is a nuanced interaction that goes past the battleground. Competitors should adjust to the group's way of life, figure out the instructing reasoning, and fashion associations with partners, training staff, and the board. The elements of group activities put an exceptional on science and union, and the capacity to fit consistently into the group dynamic is a vital part of an effective combination.

Joining an expert group frequently includes migrating to another city or nation, adding one more layer of intricacy to the progress. Competitors should explore the difficulties of adjusting to another culture, conceivably learning another dialect, and laying out an emotionally supportive network in a new climate. The off-field changes are vital to the general incorporation process, adding to the competitor's general prosperity and, thusly, their exhibition on the field.

Mentors assume a vital part in the combination cycle, giving direction, setting assumptions, and working with the competitor's osmosis into the group. They frequently go about as tutors, assisting competitors with exploring the complexities of expert play, giving experiences into strategic subtleties, and offering an emotionally supportive network that reaches out past the battleground. The connection between a mentor and a recently joined competitor is essential in molding the underlying phases of their expert process.

The primary instructional courses and communications with colleagues mark the functional commencement into the expert group. Competitors should rapidly check the playing styles, correspondence designs, and the general ethos of the group. The power of expert preparation is much of the time raised, expecting competitors to stretch their actual boundaries and show their availability for the afflictions of serious play. The versatility and learning nimbleness of the competitor are tried as they retain new techniques, strategies, and positional obligations.

The presentation coordinate with the expert group is a snapshot of extraordinary importance. Whether it's venturing onto the field, court, or pitch, the competitor's presentation is investigated by the instructing staff as well as by fans, media, and rivals. The presentation addresses the primary chance for the competitor to grandstand their abilities in the expert field, and it frequently establishes the vibe for their residency with the group.

The tension related with the introduction is unmistakable. Competitors should fight with the assumptions for fans, the heaviness of addressing the expert group, and the longing to have a quick effect. The capacity to deal with this tension, keep fixed on the strategy, and convey a presentation that lines up with the group's targets is a demonstration of the competitor's psychological determination and versatility.

Outcome in the presentation match is a certainty sponsor, for the competitor as well as for the group and its allies. It lays out the competitor as a sound supporter of the group's targets and hardens their situation inside the crew. On the other hand, difficulties or mishaps in the presentation match become open doors for development, requiring strength, self-reflection, and a pledge to consistent improvement.

The brotherhood created with colleagues is an indispensable part of the mix interaction. Group activities flourish with correspondence, common comprehension, and an aggregate quest for progress. Competitors should explore the relational elements inside the group, fabricate compatibility with partners, and contribute emphatically to the general group culture. The capacity to cultivate solid associations with individual players makes a strong unit that can explore the intricacies of expert rivalry.

Off-field liabilities additionally become possibly the most important factor as competitors join proficient groups. Media commitment, sponsorship responsibilities, and local area outreach exercises become essential pieces of the competitor's daily schedule. The competitor's picture and lead off the field add to the general brand of the expert group. Adjusting these off-field commitments with thorough preparation and rivalry plans demands successful using time productively and versatility.

The effect of joining an expert group stretches out past the singular competitor to the more extensive wearing local area. It fortifies fans, adds fervor to the group's story, and adds to the general exhibition of the game. The competitor turns into a delegate of themselves as well as of the group, conveying the obligation of maintaining the group's qualities and goals.

The excursion of joining an expert group isn't without its difficulties. Competitors might experience times of change, face contest for playing time, or explore the intricacies of group elements. Wounds, a steady danger in the realm of sports, may represent extra obstacles. The capacity to defeat these difficulties, remain fixed on long haul objectives, and keep a versatile mentality is urgent for supported progress in the expert field.

Joining an expert group isn't the finish of the excursion yet the start of another section in a competitor's vocation. The residency with an expert group is set apart by constant development, improvement, and the quest for greatness. Competitors should remain sensitive to developing systems, adjust to changes in the group dynamic, and reliably show their worth to the crew. The excursion turns into a recurrent course of refinement, where each match, each instructional meeting, and every connection add to the competitor's development.

2. **First taste of elite competition**

The main taste of world class rivalry is a pivotal occasion in the profession of a competitor, a second that rises above the limits of simple support and denotes the section into a domain where expertise, commitment, and flexibility are tried at the most significant level. This critical crossroads frequently comes because of advancing through formative stages, procuring a spot in public crews, or getting a situation in renowned competitions or associations. It is a perfection of long periods of difficult work, penance, and immovable obligation to the game.

For some competitors, the excursion to world class rivalry starts in the cauldron of youth and formative associations. These associations act as hatcheries for ability, giving a stage to youthful competitors to feature their abilities and grab the eye of scouts, mentors, and ability spotters. The progress from these formative stages to first class contest is a demonstration of a competitor's ability, potential, and status for the difficulties that anticipate at the most noteworthy echelons of their game.

The hit up to public crews is a crucial second in a competitor's excursion. Addressing one's country on the global stage isn't just an honor yet additionally a significant obligation. Public group determinations frequently accompany elevated assumptions, as competitors are entrusted with exemplifying the aggregate yearnings and pride of their country. The first taste of world class rivalry in quite a while turns into a wellspring of gigantic pride and an impression of the competitor's remaining in the worldwide wearing scene.

Getting a situation in esteemed competitions or associations is one more pathway to world class contest. Whether it's the Olympics, a World Cup, a Huge homerun occasion, or a high-profile association, these contests address the zenith of sports. Competitors who procure the chance to take part in such occasions experience a seismic change in the force and stakes of rivalry. The principal appearance on these great stages is a perfection of dreams and an approval of the competitor's excursion.

The expectation paving the way to the primary taste of first class rivalry is substantial. Competitors go through thorough arrangement, tweaking their abilities, concentrating on rivals, and guaranteeing top physical and mental molding. Mentors assume a significant part during this stage, giving key direction, imparting certainty, and assisting competitors with exploring the novel difficulties presented by first class rivalry. The planning reaches out past the actual space to incorporate mental status for the tensions and assumptions that accompany contending at the most elevated level.

The second a competitor ventures onto the field, court, track, or field for their most memorable taste of tip top contest is a combination of nerves, energy, and a profound feeling of direction. The thunder of the group, the public songs of praise playing, or the notorious settings make an air that is both jolting and lowering. For group activities, the common involvement in colleagues enhances the meaning existing apart from everything else, as competitors join under a typical pennant to address their nation or club.

In individual games, the initial introduction to world class contest is a singular yet significant experience. Competitors remain solitary, their abilities and readiness tried in the pot of contest. The quest for individual greatness becomes the dominant focal point, and the main taste of tip top rivalry turns into a marker in the competitor's very own mission for significance.

The force of world class contest is portrayed by the degree of expertise showed as well as by the psychological backbone expected to perform under tension. A lot is on the line, and the edge for blunder is thin. Competitors should explore the mental difficulties of tip top rivalry, remaining on track, strong, and versatile despite unexpected conditions. The capacity to stay under control and execute systems in the midst of the cauldron of world class rivalry is a main quality of fruitful competitors.

For group activities, the cooperative energy among colleagues turns into a significant consider exploring first class rivalry. Correspondence, trust, and a mutual perspective of jobs and obligations add to the aggregate exertion. Competitors should rapidly adjust to the elements of world class play, figuring out the subtleties of resistance systems, and executing their approach with accuracy. The attachment manufactured during instructional meetings is placed to the test on the stupendous phase of world class contest.

The principal taste of first class rivalry frequently accompanies an acknowledgment of the raised norm and the degree of contest. Competitors witness firsthand the abilities of their friends, the complexities of cutting edge procedures, and the persistent speed of play. This openness turns into a learning an open door, offering experiences into the benchmarks of greatness and propelling competitors to refine their abilities consistently.

Triumphs in tip top rivalry are commended as achievements, for the singular competitor as well as for the whole group or country. The happiness of progress, the celebration of accomplishing a long-looked for objective, and the common euphoria among colleagues make recollections that persevere past the limits of the battleground. These triumphs become piece of the aggregate account, adding to the tradition of the group or country in tip top contest.

On the other hand, mishaps and difficulties in world class rivalry become examples in strength and determination. Routs, while without a doubt disheartening, offer open doors for reflection, improvement, and development. Competitors should explore the profound lows, return from misfortunes, and channel affliction into fuel for future achievement. The excursion of first class contest is described by the two victories and hardships, and the competitor's reaction to challenges shapes their personality.

The effect of the main taste of world class contest stretches out past the quick outcomes. It impacts a competitor's direction, molding their goals, and powering a want supported achievement. Competitors frequently discuss the groundbreaking idea of world class contest, how it modifies their viewpoint, imparts a more prominent feeling of direction, and moves them to take a stab at much more prominent levels in their vocations.

The kinship created with colleagues during world class rivalry makes bonds that stretch out past the battleground. Shared encounters, triumphs, and even losses manufacture associations that become the bedrock of group union. Partners become something beyond associates; they become companions, comrades, and mainstays of help during the ups and downs of a competitor's excursion.

The main taste of tip top rivalry likewise hoists a competitor's perceivability on the worldwide stage. Exhibitions in lofty competitions or associations accumulate consideration from fans, media, and backers. Competitors who leave an imprint in first class contest frequently wind up at the center of attention, becoming representatives for their game and rousing the up and coming age of competitors. The impact stretches out past the domain of game, with competitors utilizing their foundation to advocate for purposes, add to cultural change, and shape discussions on and off the field.

5.2 Establishing a Presence

Laying out a presence in the realm of sports is a multi-layered try that goes past on-field execution. It includes building an individual brand, drawing in with fans, adding to the local area, and exploring the intricacies of the games business. Competitors, mentors, and sports characters perceive the significance of succeeding in their picked discipline as well as making a personality that reverberates with a more extensive crowd.

The most common way of laying out a presence frequently starts with the improvement of an individual brand. Competitors are presently not simply contenders; they are brands regardless of anyone else's opinion. The formation of an unmistakable individual brand includes a smart curation of one's picture, values, and yearnings. This brand turns into a special identifier, separating the competitor and making an association with fans. Components like individual style, virtual entertainment presence, and off-field exercises add to the molding of this brand.

Drawing in with fans is a foundation of laying out a presence in the games world. Fans are not simply onlookers; they are a local area that frames the heartbeat of any game. Competitors perceive the meaning of fan commitment, utilizing web-based entertainment stages, fan occasions, and local area drives to associate with their allies. The capacity to manufacture a certified association with fans cultivates reliability, makes a feeling of having a place, and raises the competitor's remaining according to people in general.

Web-based entertainment, specifically, has turned into an integral asset for competitors to lay out and enhance their presence. Stages like Instagram, Twitter, and TikTok give an immediate channel to competitors to share their characters, experiences, and in the background minutes. Competitors utilize these stages not exclusively to exhibit their accomplishments on the field yet additionally to offer a brief look into their lives off the field. Genuineness and appeal in virtual entertainment commitment add to the refinement of competitors, making them more available and charming to fans.

Past individual competitors, groups and associations likewise perceive the benefit of developing areas of strength for a presence. Web-based entertainment fills in as a course for groups to interface with their fan base, share refreshes, and make a computerized local area around the group's personality. The cooperative energy between individual competitors' very own brands and the aggregate brand of a group makes a powerful story that resounds with different crowds.

Local area contribution is one more road through which competitors lay out a significant presence. Perceiving the impact they use, numerous competitors effectively participate in magnanimity, social causes, and local area administration.

Past being good examples on the field, competitors become envoys for positive change off the field. Drives, for example, good cause occasions, outreach projects, and associations with philanthropic associations add to the competitor's inheritance and effect past the domain of sports.

The foundation of a presence likewise includes exploring the business side of sports. Competitors frequently become endorsers, marking sponsorship bargains, and turning into the essence of brands. These organizations contribute not exclusively to the competitor's monetary portfolio yet in addition to their perceivability in the business scene. Arranging support bargains, overseeing brand connections, and understanding the complexities of the games business environment become fundamental abilities in laying out an enduring presence.

Media commitment assumes an essential part in forming a competitor's public persona. Interviews, question and answer sessions, and media appearances give potential open doors to competitors to verbalize their viewpoints, share bits of knowledge, and add to the more extensive story of their game. Media cooperations permit competitors to discuss straightforwardly with fans, address debates, and present a firm story that lines up with their own image.

The foundation of a presence isn't without its difficulties. Competitors might confront investigation, analysis, and the tensions of public assumptions. The capacity to explore the spotlight with effortlessness, answer difficulties with strength, and keep up with respectability notwithstanding outer tensions turns into a demonstration of a competitor's personality. Media preparing, advertising methodologies, and a solid emotionally supportive network assume essential parts in assisting competitors with enduring the intricacies of public consideration.

The worldwide idea of sports implies that competitors frequently wind up addressing their singular brands as well as their nations or groups on the global stage. Public group call-ups, support in worldwide competitions, and the chance to contend in esteemed associations add to a competitor's presence on the worldwide scale. The exhibitions on this worldwide stage become pivotal turning points that add layers to the competitor's story and add to their remaining in the more extensive games local area.

The foundation of a presence isn't restricted to players alone; mentors, pundits, and sports characters likewise participate all the while. Mentors, specifically, assume a crucial part in forming the character of a group and adding to the story of progress. The allure and relational abilities of observers become fundamental to the watcher's insight, adding variety to the narrating of games. Each figure in the games environment adds to the general embroidery of presence that characterizes the business.

Difficulties, debates, and misfortunes are unavoidable in the excursion of laying out a presence. Competitors should fight with wounds, execution droops, and the always present apparition of public examination. How competitors answer difficulty turns into an essential part of their presence. Straightforwardness, modesty, and a pledge to ceaseless improvement add to the flexibility that characterizes getting through sports figures.

The idea of laying out a presence reaches out to the more extensive games industry, incorporating associations, overseeing bodies, and sports establishments. The standing of an association, the straightforwardness of administration, and the inclusivity of strategies all add to the general picture of the games biological system. Sports foundations perceive the need to develop with cultural changes, address issues of variety and consideration, and encourage a culture that lines up with contemporary qualities.

1. **Skill development and honing expertise**

    Expertise improvement and the sharpening of skill address a nonstop and fundamental part of a singular's process in any field, yet especially so in the domain of sports. The quest for greatness in sports requests natural ability as well as a steady obligation to refining and growing one's range of abilities. Competitors, mentors, and sports experts participate in an unending pattern of picking up, preparing, and dominance to remain at the front of their particular disciplines.

At the core of expertise improvement lies the acknowledgment that capability in sports isn't static; it is a dynamic and developing cycle. Competitors leave on their brandishing venture with a groundwork of essential abilities, sharpened through long stretches of work on, instructing, and rivalry at different levels. Be that as it may, the progress from novice to first class levels requires a more profound and more nuanced comprehension of the complexities of the game.

For competitors, the excursion of expertise improvement starts early in life, frequently in grassroots projects and youth foundations. These early years act as a basic stage for gaining central abilities like coordination, deftness, and essential methods well defined for their picked sport. Mentors assume an essential part during this developmental period, conferring information, ingraining discipline, and supporting an affection for the game.

As competitors progress through the formative stages, the focal point of ability improvement grows to incorporate high level strategies, strategic discernment, and positional mindfulness. Instructional courses become more particular, with a sharp accentuation on refining explicit parts of the game. For instance, a soccer player might zero in on ball control, passing precision, and vital situating, while a tennis player might devote broad hours to culminating their serve and dominating different strokes.

The approach of innovation has fundamentally expanded the scene of ability improvement in sports. Video examination, biomechanics, and information driven experiences give competitors a more significant comprehension of their exhibitions. Mentors use these instruments to distinguish areas of progress, tailor preparing projects, and deal customized criticism to upgrade a competitor's abilities. This reconciliation of innovation into sports preparing addresses a change in perspective, empowering a more logical and designated way to deal with expertise improvement.

Notwithstanding specialized abilities, mental and profound viewpoints assume a vital part in a competitor's excursion of mastery. The capacity to remain on track under tension, settle on split-subsequent options, and deal with feelings during serious rivalry are features of a balanced competitor. Mental molding programs, sports brain research, and care procedures are progressively incorporated into preparing regimens to encourage strength, fixation, and a positive outlook.

The job of mentors stretches out past bestowing specialized information; they are instrumental in directing a competitor's general turn of events. Mentors act as coaches, inspirations, and vital planners, formulating preparing plans that line up with a competitor's assets and areas of progress.

The mentorship angle is especially essential, as mentors give specialized mastery as well as offer the vital help and direction to explore the difficulties inborn in seeking after greatness in sports.

The quest for mastery in sports frequently includes looking for motivation from unbelievable figures and gaining from their excursions. Competitors concentrate on the methods, systems, and outlooks of famous games characters to gather experiences that can be applied to their own turn of events. These good examples become reference points of greatness, representing the conceivable outcomes of expertise dominance and filling in as a wellspring of inspiration for those trying to arrive at the zenith of their game.

While the beginning phases of expertise advancement center around the securing of central capacities, the change to first class levels requests a pledge to consistent improvement. This involves a mentality of unending realizing, where competitors continually examine their exhibitions, recognize regions for improvement, and team up with mentors to configuration designated preparing programs. The most achieved competitors comprehend that mastery is an excursion, not an objective, and they embrace the continuous course of refinement.

Specialization is a typical subject in expertise improvement, especially as competitors progress to more elevated levels of contest. As sports become more professionalized, competitors frequently level up their abilities in unambiguous positions or parts of the game. For example, a b-ball player might have some expertise in three-point shooting, a swimmer in a specific stroke, or a track competitor in a particular occasion.

This specialization permits competitors to use their one of a kind qualities and contribute fundamentally to their groups or succeed independently.

Preparing philosophies additionally develop pair with headways in sports science. Periodization, which includes arranging preparing cycles to improve execution during top periods, has turned into a standard practice in sports preparing. This deliberate methodology guarantees that competitors go through periods of extreme preparation, trailed by times of rest and recuperation, prompting upgraded physical and mental readiness for contest.

Expertise improvement reaches out past the domains of actual ability; it envelops a profound comprehension of the strategic subtleties of the game. Group activities, specifically, request an aggregate dominance of methodologies, blueprints, and successful correspondence among partners. Mentors assume a urgent part in granting these strategic bits of knowledge, cultivating a firm comprehension among players, and refining the group's general exhibition.

The quest for mastery in sports isn't without its difficulties. Competitors frequently wrestle with wounds, execution levels, and the psychological strain related with high-stakes rivalry. Conquering these deterrents requires flexibility, versatility, and a guarantee to the restoration and recuperation processes. The capacity to explore misfortunes and use them as venturing stones for development is a sign of competitors who persistently develop in their excursion of mastery.

For mentors, keeping up to date with developing training techniques, sports science research, and innovative headways is vital for guide competitors really. Proficient improvement for mentors isn't just supported however has turned into a need in a scene where the edge among progress and unremarkableness can be razor-slight. Instructing schooling programs, mentorship drives, and cooperative stages empower mentors to refine their strategies and give ideal direction to competitors.

The excursion of skill in sports is set apart by achievements that mirror a competitor's movement. Accomplishments like coming out on top for titles, breaking records, and procuring awards are unmistakable signs of a competitor's authority. Nonetheless, the elusive perspectives, like authority characteristics, sportsmanship, and the capacity to rouse partners, are similarly huge in laying out a tradition of greatness.

The idea of conscious practice, advocated by clinician Anders Ericsson, highlights the significance of deliberate and centered preparing in expertise advancement. Competitors took part in purposeful practice effectively search out difficulties that push their limits, get prompt and enlightening criticism, and reliably refine their procedures. This purposeful way to deal with preparing separates those on the way to aptitude from the individuals who just make a cursory effort.

The adaptability of abilities across various settings is a captivating part of skill in sports. Competitors who have dominated explicit abilities frequently track down that the standards of discipline, determination, and key reasoning are relevant in different parts of their lives. The abilities sharpened in the pot of sports become fundamental abilities that add to self-improvement and accomplishment past the bounds of the battleground.

2. **Gaining recognition on the national stage**

Earning respect on the public stage is a turning point in the excursion of any competitor. It addresses the zenith of long stretches of difficult work, devotion, and expertise advancement, flagging individual accomplishment as well as the affirmation of one's ability inside the more extensive donning local area of their country. This acknowledgment isn't just an individual accomplishment;

it lifts the competitor to a place of impact, moving others and adding to the aggregate story of the game.

For some competitors, the way to public acknowledgment starts at the grassroots level. Youth contests, school competitions, and provincial titles act as the underlying stages where maturing gifts grandstand their abilities. Mentors, scouts, and ability spotters effectively screen these occasions, distinguishing promising competitors whose potential can be sustained and created. The progress from neighborhood contests to public unmistakable quality frequently depends on champion exhibitions that catch the consideration of the people who assume a part in ability recognizable proof.

Public acknowledgment is naturally attached to cooperation in public groups or crews. Competitors who get call-ups to address their country on the global stage experience a change in outlook with regards to perceivability and assumptions. Public group choices are a demonstration of a competitor's reliable exhibitions, expertise level, and capacity to add to the aggregate objectives of the group. The distinction of wearing the public tones turns into a wellspring of huge pride, both for the competitor and their local area.

The public stage furnishes competitors with openness to more elevated levels of rivalry and a really insightful crowd. Whether it's contending in public titles, addressing the country in global competitions, or taking part in esteemed associations, these encounters contribute essentially to a competitor's profile. Accomplishment on the public stage frequently includes individual accomplishments as well as the capacity to perform under the tension of addressing one's country.

Media assumes a vital part in enhancing a competitor's presence on the public stage. Transmissions, paper articles, and online inclusion carry the competitor's exhibitions to a more extensive crowd, transforming them into commonly recognized names.

Competitors become subjects of meetings, elements, and profiles, permitting people in general to associate with their accounts, battles, and wins. Media inclusion turns into a situation with two sides, presenting competitors to both praise and investigation.

Public acknowledgment isn't restricted to the brandishing field; it stretches out to honors, grants, and respects that insist a competitor's remaining inside the country. Grants, for example, "Player of the Year," acceptances into sports corridors of distinction, and public games praises are unmistakable appearances of a competitor's commitments to their game. These awards celebrate individual greatness as well as act as a motivation desiring competitors, supporting the idea that difficult work and devotion are properly compensated.

The effect of earning respect on the public stage rises above the singular competitor; it impacts the view of the actual game. Effective competitors become ministers for their game, causing to notice its subtleties, fervor, and social importance. The stories made around competitors add to the general picture of the game, forming the way things are seen by people in general, media, and possible backers.

Acknowledgment on the public stage frequently opens ways to support open doors and sponsorship bargains. Companies and brands try to fall in line with effective competitors, utilizing their ubiquity to upgrade their own picture. Supports give monetary advantages to the competitors as well as add to their perceivability, permitting them to broaden their impact past the bounds of the battleground.

The obligation that accompanies public acknowledgment stretches out to being a good example for hopeful competitors and the more extensive local area. Competitors know that their activities, both on and off the field, are firmly examined. They become images of assurance, flexibility, and sportsmanship, exemplifying qualities that stretch out past the domain of sports. The effect of a positive good example can be significant, motivating the cutting edge to seek after their fantasies with force and honesty.

While earning respect on the public stage is a snapshot of win, it likewise presents new difficulties and assumptions. Competitors should explore the tensions of uplifted investigation, expanded contest, and the heaviness of public assumptions. The capacity to deal with progress with lowliness, oversee outside tensions, and keep fixed on ceaseless improvement becomes basic for those looking for persevering through progress.

Instructing and mentorship keep on assuming essential parts even after a competitor earns respect on the public stage. Mentors guide competitors in exploring the intricacies of more significant level contest, refining their abilities, and adjusting to developing procedures. Mentorship from experienced competitors who have track a comparable way gives important bits of knowledge and an emotionally supportive network that facilitates the progress to the requests of public noticeable quality.

The effect of earning respect on the public stage is in many cases felt past the lines of the games field. Competitors become social symbols, addressing athletic ability as well as typifying the soul of their country. Their accounts become entwined with the more extensive story of the nation, adding to a feeling of public pride and solidarity. The competitor's victories and difficulties become shared encounters that reverberate with fans across different socioeconomics.

CHAPTER 6

Trials and Triumphs

Preliminaries and wins are fundamental parts of the many-sided embroidered artwork woven through a competitor's excursion. This convincing account unfurls against the setting of difficulties that test a competitor's strength, constancy, and mental backbone. The preliminaries looked in the pot of contest, individual snags, and the quest for greatness are offset snapshots of win, where the sweet taste of triumph turns into the perfection of enduring devotion and unyielding soul.

The preliminaries that competitors experience frequently manifest on the serious stage, where the journey for progress is loaded with obstructions. Misfortune takes many structures — imposing adversaries, surprising mishaps, and the unrelenting strain to perform. Competitors explore the intricacies of high-stakes rivalries, where the edge among triumph and rout is razor-slim. The psychological and profound cost of confronting savage contest, combined with the actual requests of the game, shapes a competitor's personality and characterizes their determination.

In group activities, the elements of cooperation and relationship present an extra layer of intricacy to the preliminaries looked by competitors. The capacity to synchronize endeavors with partners, convey consistently, and adjust to the ease of the game becomes foremost. Preliminaries in group activities frequently stretch out past individual execution to aggregate difficulties like group union, key arrangement, and the ability to defeat shortfalls. Wins in group activities convey a collective reverberation, with triumphs celebrated as shared accomplishments that tight spot partners in an embroidery of common perspective.

Individual preliminaries entwine with the athletic excursion, as competitors face the innate weaknesses of the human experience. Wounds, difficulties, and the toil of thorough preparation regimens present considerable difficulties. Competitors wrestle with the dissatisfaction of sidelined goals, the anguish of actual agony, and the mental cost of restoration. Beating individual preliminaries requires a mix of strength, persistence, and a tenacious obligation to the rehabilitative cycle. The ability to change mishaps into potential open doors for development turns into a sign of competitors who rise up out of private preliminaries more grounded and stronger.

The quest for greatness itself is a determined preliminary that requests enduring devotion, penance, and a resolute hard working attitude. Competitors explore the fine harmony between pushing actual limits and staying balanced. The mission for persistent improvement impels competitors into an unending pattern of preparing, examination, and variation. Wins chasing after greatness are not bound to platform gets done; they manifest in the refinement of abilities, the achievement of individual outmaneuvers, and the determined quest for one's maximum capacity.

Preliminaries stretch out past the actual domain, penetrating the psychological and profound components of a competitor's insight. The strain to measure up to outer assumptions, the examination of media and fans, and the interior drive for flawlessness make a cauldron where mental versatility is essentially as vital as actual ability. Competitors frequently work with sports clinicians to develop mental grit, survival techniques, and a positive outlook that empowers them to explore the mental difficulties inborn in world class rivalry.

The cooperative connection among preliminaries and wins becomes clear in the rhythmic movement of a competitor's vocation. Difficulties prepare for rebounds, and snapshots of rout become impetuses for future triumphs. The account curve of a competitor's process isn't straight; it is a powerful interaction among pinnacles and valleys, each adding to the general story of versatility and win.

Wins, when they happen, are the crescendo in the ensemble of a competitor's excursion. They emerge as platform gets done, title triumphs, and the acknowledgment of long-esteemed dreams.

The flavor of win isn't simply the fulfillment of individual accomplishment; it is the perfection of penances made, challenges survive, and the tireless quest for greatness. Triumphs become waypoints in the competitor's account, markers that accentuate the exhausting excursion with snapshots of happiness and confirmation.

The meaning of wins reaches out past individual satisfaction; it resonates through the competitor's emotionally supportive network and the more extensive local area. Family, mentors, partners, and fans share in the delight of win, their commitments woven into the texture of the competitor's prosperity. Wins become common festivals, rising above individual achievements to represent aggregate accomplishment and the versatility of the human soul.

In group activities, the euphoria of wins is amplified as colleagues meet up to loll in the brilliance of shared achievement. Title triumphs, unequivocal triumphs against imposing opponents, and the acknowledgment of group objectives become permanent parts in the aggregate story of the group. The securities produced through preliminaries become the bedrock whereupon wins are commended, making a fellowship that stretches out past the battleground.

Wins on the public stage raise a competitor to famous status inside the social story of their country. Title triumphs, record-breaking exhibitions, and snapshots of magnificence in global contests become a wellspring of public pride. Competitors change into social images, exemplifying the goals, flexibility, and wins of their country. The effect of these victories reaches out past the brandishing field, impacting the aggregate mind and encouraging a feeling of solidarity and character.

Individual victories in defeating difficulty, whether as wounds, individual mishaps, or the toil of thorough preparation, are similarly significant. The flexibility showed notwithstanding preliminaries turns into a wellspring of motivation for others confronting difficulties. Competitors who share their accounts of win over difficulty become encouraging signs, showing that mishaps are not unrealistic obstructions but rather venturing stones to more prominent levels.

Wins chasing greatness frequently involve breaking boundaries and setting new benchmarks. Competitors who break records, rethink prospects, and accomplish accomplishments recently considered out of reach become pioneers inside their game. These victories add to the advancement of the actual game, moving people in the future to push limits and outperform the restrictions of what is thought of as feasible.

The tradition of a competitor is complicatedly attached to their victories, as these snapshots of greatness shape how they are recollected in the archives of sports history. Famous competitors leave a permanent engraving through their victories, making an enduring inheritance that rises above the transient idea of cutthroat professions. The story of wins turns into a story went down through ages, moving hopeful competitors to take a stab at significance and helping the world to remember the persevering through force of the human soul.

Preliminaries and wins are not secluded occasions but rather interconnected strings woven into the texture of a competitor's excursion. The juxtaposition of difficulties and triumphs makes a story that is both convincing and full. Competitors who explore preliminaries with effortlessness and arise victorious become living epitomes of the versatility, constancy, and unfaltering soul that characterize the substance of sports. The preliminaries are the cauldron where character is fashioned, and the victories are the delegated minutes that enlighten the way of a competitor's excursion, making a permanent imprint on the scene of sports history.

6.1 High-Stakes Matches

High-stakes matches stand as vital points in the vocations of competitors, minutes when the power of rivalry arrives at its apex and the result resounds a long ways past the bounds of the battleground. These challenges, frequently portrayed by raised pressure, elevated assumptions, and the quest for critical titles or awards, embody the pith of sports show. Competitors who end up in high-stakes matches explore a territory where the edges among triumph and rout are razor-slender, and the effect stretches out past private accomplishment to shape heritages, characterize professions, and engraving permanent minutes in the aggregate memory of fans.

One principal trait of high-stakes matches is the heaviness of assumptions that goes with them. Competitors, mentors, and groups participate in these challenges conveying the desires of fans, the examination of media, and the weight of their own aspirations. The size of the event intensifies the strain, changing the opposition into a cauldron where the grit of contenders is tried. The capacity to deal with these assumptions, channel tension into concentration, and adapt to the situation turns into a sign of competitors who flourish in high-stakes conditions.

Title finals, title-choosing matches, and challenges with huge season finisher suggestions are model instances of high-stakes matches. These experiences address the perfection of a season of exertion, commitment, and diligence. The story circular segment of an association or competition combines into a solitary, unequivocal second, where the result has enduring ramifications for the competitors in question, their groups, and the more extensive games scene. The expectation paving the way to these matches is discernible, and the stakes are raised by the information that achievement or disappointment will be carved into the records of sports history.

The elevated show of high-stakes matches frequently comes from the conflict of considerable rivals — groups or people who have navigated a moving excursion to arrive at the zenith of rivalry. These matches highlight the assembly of greatness, where the best strive against the best. The cutthroat harmony is sensitive, and the result is questionable, adding an additional layer of interest and fervor for fans. The accounts of longstanding contentions, battles, and notable showdowns are woven into the texture of high-stakes challenges, implanting them with close to home reverberation.

Individual competitors end up in high-stakes matches that can characterize their professions and shape their heritages. Huge homerun finals in tennis, title sessions in boxing, and Olympic decoration rivalries address particular minutes where a competitor's collection of work is refined into a represent the moment of truth situation. The strain to convey a champion presentation, jump all over the opportunity, and engraving one's name in the pantheon of sports greats is discernible. The versatility and mental mettle expected to explore such circumstances become characterizing ascribes of competitors who arise triumphant.

Group activities, then again, exhibit the aggregate elements of high-stakes matches. The mind boggling interaction of techniques, the cooperative energy of collaboration, and the common obligation of accomplishing a shared objective add layers of intricacy to these challenges. Title games in sports like soccer, ball, and cricket hoist group accomplishments to a pinnacle where the attachment of the gathering is tried under the unforgiving spotlight of high-stakes contest. The story bend of a season comes full circle in a crescendo of feeling, where the bond produced among partners is uncovered for all to observe.

The show of high-stakes matches stretches out past the players on the field to include the job of mentors and planners. The choices made uninvolved, the changes in accordance with strategies, and the capacity to peruse the back and forth movement of the challenge become essential components that can steer the results for one side. Mentors should explore the sensitive harmony between reasonable courses of action and vital traditionalism, settling on split-subsequent options that can impact the direction of the match. The essential chess match between training staff adds an extra layer of interest to high-stakes experiences.

The appeal of high-stakes matches lies in the erratic story circular segments they make. The dark horse prevailing against overpowering chances, the surprising legend arising in a crucial point in time, and the story turns that oppose assumptions — these components add to the immortal allure of sports show. The profound rollercoaster experienced by fans, from celebration to tragedy, mirrors the soothing force of high-stakes matches that tap into the basic quintessence of rivalry.

One of the persevering through traditions of high-stakes matches is the production of notable minutes that rise above the prompt setting of the opposition. These minutes become piece of the games dictionary, referred to and remembered by fans and savants the same. The last-minute objectives, signal beating shots, and sensational rebounds draw themselves into the aggregate memory, becoming persevering through images of the unusual excellence of sports. The reverberation of these minutes reaches out past the domain of measurements and titles; they become social standards implanted in the shared perspective.

The effect of high-stakes matches resounds through the vocations of competitors. As far as some might be concerned, these challenges address the unparalleled accomplishments that characterize their inheritance. Triumphs in title finals, gold award exhibitions, and title-securing minutes become the apex of a competitor's group of work. The feeling of achievement, the delight of imparted accomplishment to colleagues, and the approval of long stretches of commitment make these triumphs groundbreaking achievements in a competitor's excursion.

On the other hand, the distress of rout in high-stakes matches is a significant encounter that makes a permanent imprint. The botched open doors, the frightful what-uncertainties, and the aggregate tragedy of missing the mark in an essential second become getting through recollections that competitors convey with them. However, it is many times in the pot of rout that the seeds of strength are planted, and competitors track down the inspiration to return, gain from the experience, and return more grounded in future high-stakes experiences.

High-stakes matches add to the making of sports stories that rise above the quick setting of a solitary rivalry. These stories shape the more extensive talk around sports, affecting conversations on significance, contention, and the persevering through allure of athletic rivalry. The narrating part of high-stakes matches, filled by notable minutes, close to home ups and downs, and the conflict of titans, changes sports into a rich embroidery of human show that dazzles crowds across the globe.

The worldwide idea of high-stakes matches intensifies their effect, rising above geographic limits and social contrasts. Global contests, like the FIFA World Cup, the Olympic Games, and significant tennis competitions, become fields where public pride, personality, and the common energy for sports join. The aggregate insight of observing high-stakes matches, whether in pressed arenas or through computerized stages, makes a feeling of worldwide local area where fans from different foundations are joined by the normal language of sports.

1. **Championship pursuits**

   Title pursuits stand as the peak of a competitor's desires, addressing the perfection of long periods of devotion, penance, and immovable obligation to greatness. Whether in individual games or group tries, the quest for a title typifies the quintessence of serious soul, strength, and the unstoppable will to arrive at the zenith of one's picked discipline. The excursion towards a title is a diverse story, winding around together the strings of readiness, methodology, cooperation, and the innate capriciousness of sports.

   The underpinning of a title pursuit is laid in the determined drudgery of everyday preparation, where competitors level up their abilities, fabricate perseverance, and develop the psychological mettle expected for tip top contest.

   The quest for greatness turns into a lifestyle, as competitors explore overwhelming preparation regimens, push their actual limits, and submerge themselves in a culture of persistent improvement. The obligation to the art is unfaltering, energized by the craving to remain on the platform and engraving one's name in the chronicles of sports history.

   Group elements assume a significant part in title pursuits, as competitors team up with mentors, support staff, and colleagues to produce a strong unit. The collaboration among colleagues, worked through shared encounters, trust, and powerful correspondence, turns into a foundation of progress. Title winning groups are in many cases described by an aggregate ethos that rises above individual accomplishments, where the entire is more prominent than the amount of its parts. Collaboration reaches out past the battleground to encourage a culture of flexibility, responsibility, and common help that supports the group through the ups and downs of a season.

Key keenness is a key part in title pursuits, with mentors and competitors carefully arranging their way to deal with every contest. The examination of adversaries, the advancement of approaches, and the capacity to adjust progressively during matches are fundamental parts of vital greatness. Title type groups and competitors have the prescience to expect difficulties, exploit shortcomings, and profit by valuable open doors, exhibiting a degree of strategic refinement that separates them headed for greatness.

The customary season fills in as a preface to title pursuits, with competitors and groups moving for position, refining their procedures, and picking up speed for the postseason. The stakes are raised in season finisher situations, where each match conveys the heaviness of likely disposal. The success or-return home nature of end of the season games heightens the show, as competitors face the truth that every presentation could be an unequivocal bit nearer to or further from the sought after title. Season finisher minutes become permanent parts in the account, with notable plays, bell mixers, and sensational rebounds drawing themselves into the aggregate memory of fans.

The psychological strength expected in title pursuits is highlighted by the ability to deal with pressure, explore affliction, and keep up with center in crucial points in time. Competitors frequently work with sports analysts to foster mental strength, representation procedures, and systems for dealing with the mental cost of high-stakes rivalry. The capacity to remain created under tension, bounce back from misfortunes, and perform at top levels in title situations is a sign of competitors who flourish in the cauldron of first class sports.

Individual competitors set out on title pursuits in sports where the single mission for greatness becomes the overwhelming focus. Whether in tennis, golf, or battle sports, the way to a title includes exploring a serious scene loaded with imposing rivals and the difficulties of the game's novel elements.

Title winning people have remarkable ability as well as the psychological sturdiness to explore the isolation of high-stakes rivalries where the spotlight is uniquely engaged.

In group activities, title pursuits are set apart by the excursion through a postseason glove, where the mission for a title heightens with each passing round. The kinship manufactured through the customary season turns into a wellspring of solidarity as groups explore the success or-return home situations of end of the season games. Title groups show a mix of ability, science, and versatility that empowers them to climate the difficulties of a postseason crusade and arise triumphant on the most fabulous stage.

The quest for a title is in many cases portrayed by famous competitions that add layers of story profundity to the overall story. Whether at the degree of individual competitors or groups, contentions enhance the stakes, energizing the force of rivalry and adding profound reverberation to title pursuits. Contention matchups become scenes that rise above the quick setting of a solitary game or season, becoming getting through parts in the legend of sports history.

Title pursuits are scratched with significant minutes that become the characterizing features of a competitor's or alternately group's excursion. The game-dominating shot, the last-minute objective, the title securing play — these minutes solidify in the aggregate memory of fans and turned into the permanent tradition of title winning exhibitions. The quest for such minutes turns into a main impetus, as competitors fantasy about adding to the feature reels that characterize the story of a title crusade.

The effect of title pursuits reaches out past the singular competitor or group, resounding with fans who put genuinely in the excursion. The collective experience of supporting a group or competitor as they contin-ued looking for a title makes bonds that rise above topographical limits and social contrasts. Titles become public festivals, joining fans in shared euphoria, deplorability, and the getting through faith in the otherworldly force of sports to motivate and enrapture.

The slippery idea of titles adds a component of unusualness to title pursuits. Competitors should explore the inborn vulnerabilities of sports, where disturbs, longshot stories, and surprising turns are woven into the texture of rivalry. The erratic idea of titles adds to the immortal charm of sports, where the dark horse's victory or the startling boss turns into a demonstration of the eccentric magnificence of athletic rivalry.

The consequence of a title pursuit is set apart by festivity, celebration, and the acknowledgment of dreams. Competitors luxuriate in the happi-ness of triumph, their process approved by a definitive accomplishment in their game.

Title festivities become notable minutes, with competitors raising prizes, confetti pouring down, and the joy of shared achievement saturating the environment. The post-title sparkle stretches out to fans, who revel in the aggregate delight of seeing their group or competitor rise to the culmination of their game.

In any case, the quest for a title isn't generally delegated with progress.

The misery of missing the mark in the last snapshots of a title journey is a significant encounter that tests the strength of competitors. Rout in a title situation leaves an enduring engraving, however it likewise turns into a cauldron for development, reflection, and the assurance to return more grounded chasing future titles. The capacity to return quickly from rout and use it as an impetus for future achievement is a demonstration of the psychological courage of competitors who view mishaps as venturing stones to more prominent accomplishments.

2. **Facing formidable opponents and adversity**

Confronting considerable rivals and difficulty is an inseparable piece of the athletic excursion, a cauldron where the fortitude of competitors is tried, and versatility turns into a main attribute. The cutthroat scene, whether in individual games or group tries, is packed with difficulties acted by adversaries who stand like imposing boundaries to progress. Also, the excursion is loaded down with unanticipated difficulties — be it wounds, mishaps, or unforeseen hindrances — that request a competitor's capacity to adjust, continue on, and call inward strength.

Considerable rivals, frequently portrayed by their outstanding expertise, key ability, or actual ability, present competitors with the imposing test of beating a better of contest. The possibility of confronting foes who succeed in their specialty can be both overwhelming and empowering. For individual competitors, this could mean facing a defending champ or an opponent known for their unmatched abilities. In group activities, defying a stalwart group with a background marked by predominance adds an additional layer of intricacy.

The experience with imposing adversaries goes past actual ability; it digs into the psychological and vital components of sports. Competitors should not just battle with the actual difficulties presented by prevalent rivals yet additionally explore the mental part of rivalry. The psychological guts to remain on track, conquer self-question, and execute under tension becomes foremost. Getting ready for such matchups includes a blend of actual preparation, vital examination, and mental molding to guarantee that competitors are genuinely prepared as well as intellectually versatile.

Misfortune, then again, is an innate feature of the competitor's excursion, an eccentric power that can appear in horde structures. Wounds, for example, are a consistently present danger, equipped for crashing even the most fastidiously spread out plans.

The recuperation interaction becomes an actual recovery as well as a trial of a competitor's psychological mettle, persistence, and assurance. Defeating the misfortune of injury requires discipline, strength, and a relentless obligation to restoration conventions. Competitors frequently work intimately with clinical experts and sports specialists to explore the physical and personal difficulties presented by wounds, pointing for recuperation as well as for a re-visitation of maximized operation.

Misfortunes, whether as surprising misfortunes, execution droops, or unanticipated difficulties, add to the story of a competitor's excursion. These snapshots of difficulty become emphasis focuses, testing a competitor's personality and resolve. The capacity to quickly return from mishaps, gain from disappointments, and use misfortune as an impetus for development is a sign of competitors who persevere even with difficulties. The story bend of a competitor's vocation is definitely not a straight movement however a unique exchange among wins and misfortunes, each adding to the development of the competitor's personality.

Confronting misfortune likewise involves defying one's own constraints and weaknesses. Competitors, frequently saw as paragons of solidarity, should wrestle with the human experience of uncertainty, dread, and self-addressing. The mental cost of difficulty expects competitors to develop mental flexibility, a positive outlook, and the capacity to see difficulties as any open doors for development. The excursion through misfortune turns into a groundbreaking cycle, forming a competitor's point of view, needs, and flexibility despite future difficulties.

The elements of confronting imposing rivals and difficulty are complemented in group activities, where the aggregate reaction to challenges becomes principal. Groups frequently experience times of misfortune during a season, whether through long strings of failures, unseen struggles, or outer tensions. The capacity of a group to revitalize together, support one another, and recalibrate their techniques notwithstanding difficulty characterizes the aggregate person of the gathering. Group pioneers assume a pivotal part in cultivating a positive group culture, imparting flexibility, and propelling colleagues to beat difficulties as a durable unit.

Notorious wearing minutes frequently rise up out of the pot of confronting impressive rivals and affliction. The dark horse winning against an intensely preferred rival, the last-minute rebound, and the startling upset become getting through stories that enrapture fans and typify the unstoppable soul of sports. These minutes rise above the prompt setting of a solitary contest, becoming images of human strength, assurance, and the capricious magnificence of athletic rivalry.

The groundwork for confronting considerable rivals and affliction stretches out past the physical and mental parts of preparing. Competitors should likewise develop flexibility, a quality that empowers them to change their systems, strategies, and blueprints because of the extraordinary difficulties presented by various rivals and unanticipated conditions.

The ability to think and react quickly, settle on split-subsequent options, and adjust to developing circumstances is a sign of world class competitors who flourish in the powerful climate of sports.

Confronting imposing rivals and difficulty isn't bound to the serious field; likewise a story unfurls in the preparation ground, where the everyday routine turns into a cauldron for development. Instructional meetings are planned not exclusively to upgrade actual qualities yet in addition to recreate the capricious situations that competitors could experience in genuine rivalry. Mentors assume a crucial part in establishing preparing conditions that challenge competitors, open them to differing levels of trouble, and cultivate an outlook of constant improvement.

The idea of confronting considerable rivals and difficulty reaches out to the worldwide stage, where competitors address their nations in global rivalries. Public groups frequently experience imposing rivals with different playing styles, social subtleties, and key methodologies. The capacity to adjust to the difficulties presented by worldwide rivalry, explore social contrasts, and perform on the worldwide stage turns into a demonstration of a competitor's flexibility and strength.

The account of confronting impressive adversaries and affliction crosses with the more extensive cultural setting, as competitors become images of motivation and diligence. Past the domains of sports, the accounts of competitors conquering misfortune reverberate with crowds confronting their own difficulties. Competitors, through their excursions, become wellsprings of inspiration, encapsulating the standards of versatility, assurance, and the constant quest for objectives that reach out past the battleground.

6.2 Personal Growth

Self-improvement is a significant and basic part of the competitor's excursion, an extraordinary interaction that reaches out past the domains of actual ability to incorporate the advancement of character, versatility, and an all encompassing identity. The quest for greatness in sports isn't only about accomplishing top athletic execution yet in addition about the excursion of self-revelation, personal growth, and the development of traits that rise above the battleground.

The pot of rivalry fills in as a powerful field for self-awareness, moving competitors to stand up to their limits, push past safe places, and constantly take a stab at progress. The requests of thorough preparation, high-stakes matches, and the consistently present strain to perform establish a climate that requires mental determination, discipline, and a development outlook. Competitors figure out how to explore the ups and downs of sports, utilizing mishaps as any open doors for reflection and refinement.

Difficulty, an unavoidable sidekick in the athletic excursion, turns into an impetus for self-improvement. Mishaps, whether as wounds, unforeseen losses, or execution droops, brief competitors to dive into the openings of their personality. The most common way of beating difficulty cultivates strength, mental sturdiness, and an ability to see difficulties not as unconquerable snags but rather as venturing stones to more prominent accomplishments. Competitors frequently rise up out of times of difficulty with an elevated identity mindfulness, a comprehension of their assets and shortcomings, and a versatility that reaches out a long ways past the domain of sports.

The development mentality, a fundamental idea chasing self-improvement, is imbued in the outlook of effective competitors. The conviction that capacities can be created through devotion and difficult work fills the determined quest for development. Competitors develop a mentality that embraces difficulties, endures notwithstanding mishaps, and considers work to be the way to dominance. This development outlook pervades all parts of a competitor's life, cultivating a long lasting obligation to learning, transformation, and ceaseless personal growth.

Group activities give a special setting to self-awareness, as competitors explore the complexities of coordinated effort, correspondence, and shared liability. The elements of collaboration develop relational abilities, sympathy, and a comprehension of aggregate objectives. Competitors figure out how to add to the progress of the group, putting the aggregate above individual yearnings. The bonds fashioned in the cauldron of cooperation become a wellspring of self-improvement, as competitors foster initiative abilities, figure out how to explore different characters, and add to a culture of shared regard and kinship.

The mentorship and direction given by mentors and senior partners assume a vital part in cultivating self-improvement. Mentors, frequently filling in as tutors and good examples, go past the specialized parts of the game to impart values, hard working attitude, and a feeling of direction. The direction given by experienced colleagues establishes a supporting climate for more youthful competitors, offering bits of knowledge into the subtleties of rivalry, systems for beating difficulties, and the significance of flexibility despite mishaps.

Off the field, competitors participate in exercises that add to their self-awareness and prosperity. Instructive pursuits, local area contribution, and the development of different interests give a reasonable establishment to comprehensive turn of events. Competitors frequently seek after scholarly undertakings, adjusting their obligation to sports with instructive yearnings. The capacity to shuffle scholastic obligations with the requests of sports encourages time usage abilities, discipline, and a diverse way to deal with self-improvement.

The competitor's excursion of self-awareness reaches out to the domain of character improvement. Trustworthiness, sportsmanship, and a solid moral establishment are fundamental parts of a competitor's personality. The games field turns into a proving ground for moral navigation, fair play, and the exhibit of regard for rivals and partners the same. Competitors who embody these characteristics become champions on the field as well as good examples whose character rises above the limits of sports.

The idea of self-improvement is unpredictably attached to the thought of initiative. Competitors frequently wind up in positions of authority, whether as group commanders, coaches, or local area ministers. Authority in sports includes not just the capacity to rouse and propel partners yet additionally the obligation to show others how its done. The excursion of self-improvement furnishes competitors with the characteristics of powerful initiative — compassion, relational abilities, and the capacity to explore difficulties with flexibility and beauty.

The competitor's process additionally includes the development of the capacity to appreciate individuals on a deeper level, a familiarity with one's own feelings and the capacity to explore the feelings of others. High-stakes rivalries, the tensions of execution, and the elements of group associations require close to home versatility. Competitors figure out how to oversee pressure, handle achievement and disappointment with composure, and cultivate a positive group culture that adds to individual and aggregate development.

The quest for self-improvement rises above the quick setting of sports and reaches out to the competitor's personality past the battleground. Competitors frequently wrestle with inquiries of character, self-esteem, and life past games. The course of self-disclosure includes reflection, a reassessment of needs, and the development of a feeling of direction that reaches out past athletic accomplishments. Competitors who explore this excursion with effortlessness arise as achieved contenders as well as people with a multi-layered identity.

The idea of self-awareness isn't restricted to the span of a competitor's cut-throat profession; it stretches out to the post-serious stage, where competitors change to new sections in their lives. Retirement from serious games denotes a significant snapshot of reflection and progress. Competitors draw upon the examples of self-improvement developed through their professions to explore the difficulties of progressing to new jobs, seeking after post-athletic vocations, and adding to society in different ways.

1. **Balancing fame, family, and personal life**
   Adjusting popularity, family, and individual life is a mind boggling and requesting part of a competitor's excursion, one that requires deft route through the frequently turbulent crossing point of public examination, familial commitments, and the mission for individual satisfaction.
   The rising to popularity in the realm of sports carries with it an exceptional arrangement of difficulties that reach out past the battleground, influencing a competitor's connections, way of life, and the fragile balance of their own life.

Notoriety, frequently joined by hero worship and media consideration, can be both a gift and a revile. While it gives competitors a stage to rouse, impact, and make monetary progress, it likewise opens them to uplifted public investigation and the deficiency of security. Dealing with the requests of distinction expects competitors to work out some kind of harmony between their public persona and the confidential self. The consistent spotlight requires a cognizant work to protect individual minutes from public look, saving a similarity to predictability in the midst of the hurricane of consideration.

The investigation of distinction stretches out to a competitor's family, who frequently wind up push into the public eye by affiliation. Mates, kids, and more distant family individuals become accidental members in the competitor's excursion, dependent upon media examination, popular assessment, and the difficulties of exploring life in the shadow of acclaim. Adjusting the longing for family protection with the certainty of public consideration turns into a sensitive craftsmanship that competitors and their families should dominate.

The requests of a high-profile sports vocation frequently imply that competitors burn through broadened periods from home, contending in different competitions, instructional courses, and limited time occasions. This partition from family can strain connections, expecting competitors to track down a fragile harmony between their expert responsibilities and the requirement for quality time with friends and family. The cost of physical and close to home distance turns into a common subject, requiring compelling correspondence, trust, and a common obligation to keeping up with the familial bond.

Family turns into an essential emotionally supportive network for competitors exploring the difficulties of popularity. The faithful help of friends and family gives a balancing out force in the midst of the ups and downs of a games vocation. The significance of developing areas of strength for an establishment is highlighted by the transient idea of distinction, where athletic ability might blur, however the connections supported inside the family persevere as an enduring wellspring of solidarity and comfort.

Being a parent, specifically, adds a layer of intricacy to the difficult exercise. Competitors, as well as dealing with the requests of their vocations, wrestle with the obligations and delights of being a parent. The shuffling demonstration of being both a high-profile competitor and a current parent calls for vital using time productively, the designation of obligations, and a guarantee to making significant minutes with kids. Competitors frequently become good examples in the wearing field as well as in the circle of nurturing, epitomizing upsides of discipline, diligence, and versatility for their kids.

Exploring distinction and day to day life likewise includes settling on essential conclusions about open perceivability. Competitors might decide to safeguard their families from the public eye, restricting their appearance in the media or on friendly stages. Others embrace a more open methodology, imparting looks at their everyday life to fans as an approach to refining their public picture. The choice to exhibit or safeguard one's family turns into an individual decision impacted by individual inclinations, social contemplations, and the craving to keep a similarity to predictability in the midst of the remarkable.

The sensitive harmony among distinction and family is further nuanced by the effect of web-based entertainment. Stages like Instagram, Twitter, and Facebook furnish competitors with an immediate channel to interface with fans yet additionally open them to the entanglements of online analysis and intrusion of security. The arranged idea of online entertainment profiles adds an extra layer of intricacy, as competitors explore the almost negligible difference among legitimacy and the painstakingly created picture they present to general society.

The mission for individual satisfaction in the midst of distinction and family commitments is a continuous excursion that rises above the expert domain. Competitors, similar to any people, wrestle with inquiries of personality, reason, and life past games. The quest for individual interests, side interests, and interests outside the brandishing field turns into a urgent part of keeping a balanced life. Whether it's seeking after instructive undertakings, participating in generosity, or investigating imaginative outlets, competitors track down satisfaction in expanding their interests past the limits of their athletic professions.

Emotional wellness contemplations likewise come to the very front while adjusting acclaim, family, and individual life. The tensions of execution, public assumptions, and the consistent investigation can negatively affect a competitor's psychological prosperity. Perceiving the significance of psychological well-being, competitors progressively advocate for destigmatizing psychological well-being difficulties and looking for proficient help when required. The help of family, a solid informal community, and a proactive way to deal with mental prosperity add to a stronger and adjusted way of life.

The monetary ramifications of acclaim add one more layer to the difficult exercise. Competitors, frequently in the prime of their procuring potential during their playing professions, face the test of overseeing riches, speculations, and long haul monetary security. The obligation to accommodate their families and secure a steady future requires vital monetary preparation, the direction of monetary counsels, and a pledge to pursuing reasonable choices in the midst of the bait of worthwhile supports and undertakings.

The retirement progress addresses a basic stage in the difficult exercise, as competitors explore the shift from the spotlight of their playing vocations to a post-cutthroat life. The change in accordance with another everyday practice, the investigation of profession valuable open doors outside sports, and the protection of relational peculiarities require versatility and a forward-looking outlook. Competitors who effectively change from the zenith of popularity to a satisfying post-athletic life frequently draw upon the illustrations of flexibility, self-disclosure, and the persevering through help of family.

2. **The evolution of character and leadership**

The development of character and initiative comprises a dynamic and significant part of a competitor's excursion, rising above the bounds of sports to shape people into strong, compassionate, and powerful pioneers. The cauldron of rivalry, the brotherhood of cooperation, and the bunch difficulties experienced chasing greatness add to the extraordinary cycle that characterizes the advancement of character and authority.

At the center of this advancement is the development of character — the mixture of temperances, values, and moral rules that guide a competitor's direct here and there the field. Character is produced in the cauldron of contest, where competitors are tried not just by the afflictions of preparing and the requests of high-stakes coordinates yet additionally by their moral decisions chasing triumph. The capacity to explore the intricacies of sportsmanship, fair play, and respectability establishes the groundwork for the development of character.

Difficulty, an unavoidable buddy in any athletic excursion, fills in as an impetus for character improvement. Difficulties, misfortunes, and unexpected provokes brief competitors to go up against their own weaknesses, wrestle with disillusionment, and consider their reactions to affliction. How competitors explore these snapshots of hardship shapes their personality, imparting flexibility, determination, and a promise to personal development.

The elements of cooperation contribute fundamentally to the development of character. In group activities, competitors figure out how to coincide inside an aggregate structure, where achievement is dependent upon cooperation, correspondence, and common regard. The capacity to work as a firm unit requires the development of characteristics like compassion, responsibility, and a common obligation to the group's objectives. Partners become associates on the field as well as people who add to one another's personality improvement through shared encounters, common help, and an aggregate quest for greatness.

Initiative, unpredictably laced with character, arises as a characteristic expansion of a competitor's excursion. The development of initiative is a nuanced cycle that unfurls through different phases of a competitor's vocation.

Early encounters in group activities frequently give the underlying introduction to positions of authority, as competitors take on obligations like captaincy, mentorship, or the epitome of group values. Initiative at this stage is much of the time portrayed by showing others how its done, encouraging a positive group culture, and adding to the aggregate resolve.

As competitors progress in their vocations, the development of administration takes on a more vital and compelling aspect. Competitors become pioneers on the field as well as diplomats for their games, advocates for social causes, and guides to more youthful partners. The stage managed by sports distinction gives a remarkable open door to competitors to use their impact for positive change, supporting for issues going from civil rights to natural maintainability. The development of character turns out to be unpredictably connected with the obligation to utilize one's leverage to improve society.

Individual pursuits inside group activities offer an unmistakable setting for the development of initiative. In sports like tennis or golf, where competitors contend separately yet are much of the time a piece of more extensive group structures, initiative appears in self-inspiration, self-control, and the capacity to drive individual greatness inside the system of group elements. The development of character in individual pursuits includes an elevated feeling of moral obligation, as competitors explore the isolation of rivalry while adding to the aggregate outcome of their groups.

The mentorship and direction given by mentors assume a critical part in forming the development of character and initiative. Mentors, frequently filling in as guides and good examples, grant specialized abilities as well as impart values, hard working attitude, and a feeling of direction. The harmonious connection among mentors and competitors turns into a cauldron for initiative turn of events, as competitors draw upon the insight, experience, and direction of their guides to explore the intricacies of their professions.

Off the field, competitors take part in pursuits that add to the development of character and authority. Instructive undertakings, local area contribution, and the quest for different interests encourage a balanced point of view that rises above the solitary spotlight on athletic accomplishments. Competitors who effectively look for valuable open doors for self-improvement, scholarly excitement, and commitment with more extensive cultural issues carry a profundity to their personality that reaches out past the limits of the wearing field.

The development of character and authority is additionally complicatedly attached to the idea of the ability to appreciate people on a deeper level. Competitors, working in high-pressure conditions, figure out how to explore their own feelings and grasp the feelings of colleagues, mentors, and adversaries.

The capacity to understand people on a deeper level includes the capacity to oversee pressure, convey really, and cultivate a positive group culture. Competitors who show the capacity to understand people at their core become proficient pioneers as well as powerful figures equipped for encouraging a steady and durable group climate.

The post-cutthroat period of a competitor's process denotes an impactful second in the development of character and authority. Resigning from dynamic contest expects competitors to change from the natural schedules of preparing and rivalry to new jobs, vocations, and obligations. The capacity to adjust to change, draw upon the examples learned through long stretches of athletic pursuit, and apply the standards of initiative to new undertakings turns into a demonstration of the getting through development of character.

CHAPTER 7

Legacy in the Making

Heritage in the making is a significant and unpredictable feature of a competitor's excursion, a story that rises above the accomplishments on the field to envelop the persevering through influence on the game, the local area, and people in the future. The idea of heritage is a continuous cycle, an intentional and cognizant exertion by competitors to shape the story of their commitments and impact past the limits of their cutthroat vocations.

At its center, heritage in the making is tied in with creating a story that reaches out past individual achievements, enveloping the qualities, standards, and effect that competitors look to make as a permanent imprint on the brandishing scene. The quest for greatness in sports becomes not simply an individual journey for progress but rather a promise to contributing something significant to the game and the bigger local area. Competitors, discerning of their jobs as stewards of the game, endeavor to fabricate heritages that resound with fans, move trying competitors, and add to the positive advancement of their particular games.

The components that add to heritage in the making are complex, enveloping on-field accomplishments, sportsmanship, generosity, local area commitment, and the development of a positive public picture.

On-field achievements, while a foundation of a competitor's heritage, are only one feature of the bigger embroidery. How competitors act, explore difficulties, and influence their impact off the field contributes essentially to the heritage they are currently making.

Sportsmanship, portrayed by fair play, regard for rivals, and honesty, is a critical element of heritage really taking shape. Competitors who typify the standards of sportsmanship become champions in their separate games as well as diplomats for the soul of fair contest. The tradition of sportsmanship stretches out past the battleground, impacting the way of life of the game and setting a norm for people in the future. Competitors deliberately develop a standing for fair play, understanding that their direct turns into a characterizing component of the heritage they abandon.

Magnanimity and local area commitment are strong instruments in the making of an enduring heritage. Competitors, perceptive of the stage managed the cost of by their popularity, frequently influence their impact to add to social causes, support magnanimous drives, and have a beneficial outcome on networks. The tradition of altruism reaches out past the quick effect of monetary commitments, enveloping the gradually expanding influence of rousing others to add to significant causes. Competitors become images of athletic ability as well as impetuses for positive social change.

The development of a positive public picture is unpredictably attached to heritage really taking shape. Competitors, frequently under the investigation of media and public consideration, comprehend the significance of introducing themselves as good examples. Their decisions, both on and off the field, add to the story of their personality and values. Competitors who focus on legitimacy, lowliness, and a promise to social obligation improve the positive parts of their public picture, adding to an inheritance that reverberates with fans and earns regard past the wearing domain.

The mentorship and direction given by competitors to the cutting edge assume a crucial part in the heritage really taking shape. Experienced competitors, mindful of the effect they can have on trying gifts, effectively participate in mentorship programs, training drives, and positions of authority inside sports associations. The tradition of mentorship stretches out past the quick progress of mentees, impacting the more extensive culture of sports by cultivating a feeling of brotherhood, sportsmanship, and a guarantee to greatness.

The account of heritage in the making isn't bound to the term of a competitor's serious vocation; it stretches out to the post-cutthroat stage, where competitors change to new jobs, professions, and commitments.

Retirement denotes a basic crossroads in the development of heritage, as competitors consider their total effect, the illustrations learned through their excursion, and the continuation of their commitments past the battleground. The post-serious stage turns into a chance for competitors to solidify their inheritances through tries like instructing, broadcasting, sports organization, or generous work.

The persevering through effect of a competitor's heritage is reflected in the social and authentic setting of their game. Notorious minutes, records, and accomplishments become piece of the game's aggregate memory, adding to its rich embroidered artwork. Competitors who rise above their singular personalities to become inseparable from the actual game leave a permanent inheritance that rises above ages. The heritage turns into a piece of the game's legend, motivating new gifts, energizing the enthusiasm of fans, and forming the story of the game's development.

The idea of heritage in the making additionally crosses with the competitor's social and cultural effect. Competitors, particularly the individuals who accomplish worldwide acknowledgment, become social symbols whose impact stretches out past the domain of sports. The tradition of social effect includes the competitor's commitments to breaking obstructions, testing cultural standards, and encouraging inclusivity. Competitors who utilize their foundation to resolve issues like civil rights, variety, and balance add to a heritage that reverberates in the more extensive cultural setting.

The development of heritage is a story molded by the competitor as well as by the fans and the more extensive games local area. The manner by which fans interface with competitors, praise their accomplishments, and bring the heritage forward through ages adds a layer of extravagance to the story. Competitors, conscious of the cooperative relationship with their fan base, effectively draw in with fans through online entertainment, fan occasions, and local area outreach programs, encouraging a feeling of shared possession in the heritage creation process.

The development of inheritance is definitely not a direct direction yet a unique cycle impacted by the competitor's decisions, values, and the advancing elements of the games scene. Competitors explore difficulties, misfortunes, and changing cultural assumptions, requiring flexibility and a promise to remaining consistent with their fundamental beliefs. The heritage in the making is a living story that unfurls through the competitor's vocation, developing with every accomplishment, difficulty, and commitment to the game and society.

7.1 Record-Breaking Achievements

Record-breaking accomplishments stand as a zenith in a competitor's excursion, representing individual greatness as well as the development of sports itself. The quest for breaking records addresses a union of expertise, assurance, and a tireless quest for greatness. Competitors who draw their names into the archives of history through record-breaking achievements become champions as well as pioneers who reclassify the limits of human potential and rouse ages to come.

At the core of record-breaking accomplishments is the quest for greatness, a persevering obligation to stretching past laid out boundaries and setting new benchmarks for execution. Competitors, driven by a characteristic longing for personal development and the quest for significance, leave on an excursion that includes pushing their physical and mental limits to accomplish accomplishments that were once considered impossible. The quest for records frequently includes a careful blend of preparing, methodology, and a profound comprehension of the specialized subtleties of the game.

The meaning of record-breaking accomplishments reaches out past individual brilliance to the more extensive scene of sports. Records act as benchmarks that exemplify the movement of sports over the long run, reflecting progressions in preparing approaches, gear, and the developing principles of contest. Competitors who break records add to the account of sports history, making a permanent imprint on the aggregate memory of fans and impacting the assumptions and desires of people in the future.

Records, whether in individual or group activities, range a different cluster of classes, from speed and perseverance to expertise and accuracy. In games, the quest for world records in occasions, for example, running, distance running, and field occasions typifies the constant journey for speed, strength, and deftness. Swimmers plan to break records in the pool, gymnasts look for flawlessness in their schedules, and ball players endeavor to establish scoring standards on the court. Each game brings its novel arrangement of difficulties, and record-breaking accomplishments are a demonstration of a competitor's capacity to overcome those difficulties and rethink what is viewed as conceivable.

The brain science of breaking records dives into the unpredictable interchange between aspiration, pressure, and the psychological grit expected to perform under the spotlight. Competitors, as they approach record-breaking endeavors, frequently wrestle with the heaviness of assumptions, both inner and outer. Defeating the mental hindrances related with record endeavors includes actual planning as well as a dominance of mental flexibility, center, and the capacity to perform under tension.

The quest for records is much of the time portrayed by a progression of steady enhancements, each structure upon the other until the competitor arrives at the limit of breaking a longstanding record. Competitors fastidiously investigate their exhibitions, distinguish regions for development, and adjust their preparation regimens to accomplish max operation during record endeavors. The cycle includes a sensitive harmony between stretching the boundaries and staying balanced or injury, requiring a sharp comprehension of the body's abilities and the capacity to explore the scarce difference among desire and practicality.

The memorable idea of breaking records is amplified when competitors accomplish accomplishments that were once thought unreachable. The breaking of the four-minute mile boundary by Sir Roger Handrail in 1954 stands as a notorious instance of breaking an apparent cutoff. Railing's accomplishment carved his name in history as well as broken the mental hindrance that had persevered for a really long time, moving another age of center distance sprinters to go for the gold subtle achievement.

Innovation, preparing techniques, and the advancement of sports science assume vital parts in the journey for breaking records. Progressions in gear, from cutting edge running shoes to streamlined bathing suits, add to further developed execution and the limiting of edges between existing records and new benchmarks. Competitors team up with sports researchers, nutritionists, and physiologists to streamline their preparation, recuperation, and generally groundwork for record endeavors. The cooperative energy between mechanical headways and athletic ability is a main quality of contemporary games, where breaking records includes an intermingling of human capacity and state of the art development.

The meaning of breaking records is amplified in the domain of Olympic and big showdowns. These worldwide stages become the milestones where competitors expect to draw their names ever, rising above public limits and becoming images of human accomplishment. Olympic records, world records, and title records become a definitive approval of a competitor's ability on the most excellent stage, where the eyes of the world are centered around their exhibitions.

Group activities acquaint an aggregate aspect with the quest for records, where competitors team up to accomplish achievements that mirror the co-operative energy of collaboration and individual brightness. Group accomplishments, whether concerning sequential triumphs, scoring records, or title titles, highlight the aggregate soul that characterizes the substance of group activities. Breaking records in group activities includes individual commitments as well as the synchronization of endeavors, vital preparation, and a common obligation to accomplishing significance as an aggregate unit.

The effect of record-breaking accomplishments stretches out past the quick rush of triumph to the heritage that competitors leave in the brandishing scene. Record breakers become symbols, their names always connected with the accomplishments they achieved.

The account of sports history is molded by these illuminating presences, and their records become reference focuses for estimating greatness across ages. The persevering through nature of records adds a layer of immortality to a competitor's inheritance, as fans and history specialists keep on wondering about the accomplishments that endured for an extremely long period.

The quest for breaking records additionally includes confronting the certainty of seeing one's records outperformed by people in the future. Competitors who break records comprehend that their achievements are essential for a powerful continuum, where each record is a venturing stone for the cutting edge to outperform. The capacity to smoothly acknowledge the section of records to new hands and praise the accomplishments of replacements turns into a sign of competitors who grasp the repetitive idea of sports history.

The job of administering bodies, sports associations, and against doping organizations in guaranteeing the uprightness of records is significant. The foundation of clear rules, against doping conventions, and severe testing systems adds to keeping up with the authenticity and believability of record-breaking accomplishments. Competitors who break records inside the system of fair rivalry and adherence to moral guidelines upgrade the sacredness of their achievements.

Debates encompassing execution upgrading substances and untrustworthy practices bring up issues about the genuineness of specific records. The continuous exchange about the effect of innovation, gear progressions, and the scarce difference among advancement and unreasonable benefit includes intricacy to the talk record-breaking accomplishments. Finding some kind of harmony between embracing innovative advancement and saving the embodiment of fair rivalry turns into a ceaseless test for sports specialists.

1. **Goals, assists, and accolades**

   In the mind boggling embroidery of a competitor's excursion, objectives, helps, and honors structure the dynamic strings that wind around together a story of accomplishment, commitment, and acknowledgment. Whether on the pitch, court, arena, or field, the quest for objectives and the masterfulness of helps address the quintessence of athletic ability, while honors act as unmistakable images of acknowledgment for the commitment, expertise, and effect that competitors bring to their particular games.

   Objectives, the quintessential proportion of scoring in different games, embody the unique transaction between ability, system, and sheer physicality. In soccer, the thrill of finding the rear of the net addresses the summit of complicated ball control, exact position, and the essential sharpness to take advantage of chances. Hockey sees objectives because of deft stickhandling, quick moves, and the coordination of a group's hostile endeavors.

   The ball loop turns into a representative entrance through which players exhibit their shooting ability, nimbleness, and capacity to explore guarded difficulties. Across sports, the demonstration of scoring objectives rises above mathematical measurements; it typifies the excitement of accomplishment, the aggregate celebration of colleagues, and the euphoria of fans who witness snapshots of donning brightness.

   Helps, the frequently downplayed at this point similarly vital element of athletic execution, feature the cooperative idea of group activities. In soccer, a rich through-ball laying out up an objective, in hockey a very much planned pass prompting a conclusive score, or in b-ball a sharp help going before a urgent crate — these minutes exhibit individual expertise as well as the capacity to lift colleagues and encourage an aggregate soul. Helps typify the magnanimous part of sports, where achievement isn't exclusively estimated by individual accomplishments however by the cooperative endeavors that lead to shared wins. The excellence of a help lies in the actual demonstration as well as in the collaboration it makes, producing obligations of brotherhood and supporting the thought that triumph is an aggregate pursuit.

Awards, the trees and respects gave to competitors, act as substantial markers of acknowledgment for their commitments to the game. From MVP grants to Top pick determinations, Brilliant Boots to Player of the Competition titles, honors solidify the remarkable exhibitions, administration, and effect that competitors bring to their groups and teaches. Awards become individual achievements as well as images of greatness that reverberate with fans, rouse trying competitors, and add to a competitor's getting through inheritance. The meaning of awards reaches out past the person to the more extensive story of sports history, where each honor turns into a section in the developing story of athletic accomplishment.

The quest for objectives and the organization of helps address a continuous journey for dominance, where competitors endeavor to refine their abilities, develop in their methodologies, and contribute genuinely to the outcome of their groups. Objective scorers, frequently respected for their capacity to transform open doors into focuses on the scoreboard, become the central places of hostile methodologies. The intuition to expect, the accuracy of execution, and the psychological strength to change over under tension characterize the objective scoring ability of competitors. The quest for individual objective scoring records, like arriving at hundred years of objectives in football or accomplishing an achievement in focuses scored in b-ball, turns into a powerful part of a competitor's profession, energizing inspiration and setting benchmarks for greatness.

Helps, described by vision, inventiveness, and a sharp comprehension of partners' developments, grandstand the unselfish and vital elements of a competitor's commitment. Playmakers in soccer, hockey, or b-ball become the modelers of progress, stringing passes, setting out open doors, and encouraging a smoothness in group elements.

The specialty of the help isn't just about individual brightness yet about lifting the exhibition of the whole group. Competitors who succeed in giving helps become impetuses to hostile brightness, facilitators of group union, and essential parts of their group's prosperity.

Awards, in their different structures, act as open certifications of a competitor's effect on their game. Accomplishing the situation with Most Important Player (MVP) in an association, procuring a spot in a Top pick group, or getting lofty honors like the Ballon d'Or in football or the Hart Prize in hockey — these honors are saturated with eminence and importance. They reflect individual greatness as well as the capacity to stand apart among peers, leave an enduring imprint on the game, and add to the more extensive story of athletic accomplishment. Awards raise competitors to famous status, engraving their names in the records of sports history and leaving a permanent heritage.

The quest for individual objectives and helps, while essential to a competitor's personality, is unpredictably attached to the more extensive setting of group elements. In group activities, the collaboration between objective scorers and playmakers turns into a characterizing component of progress. The connection between a striker and a midfielder in soccer, a forward and a point monitor in b-ball, or a scorer and a playmaker in hockey includes a harmonious comprehension of one another's assets, propensities, and on-field science. The union between objective scorers and those giving helps makes a powerful hostile power that rises above individual splendor, adding to the aggregate character and progress of the group.

The meaning of objectives, helps, and honors is elevated with regards to significant competitions and titles. The World Cup in soccer, the Stanley Cup Finals in hockey, the NBA Finals in ball — these stupendous stages become pots where competitors point not exclusively to grandstand their singular splendor yet to add to the greatness of their groups on the greatest stages. Objectives and aids crucial snapshots of these contests become carved in the recollections of fans, adding layers of account to the more extensive storylines of win and misfortune. Honors in significant competitions convey added notoriety, representing the capacity to sparkle when the stakes are most elevated and leaving a persevering through engrave on the tradition of competitors.

The quest for records, both individual and group based, frequently meets with the domains of objectives, helps, and awards. Breaking objective scoring records, outperforming help achievements, or gathering honors in successive seasons become aspirations that fuel a competitor's drive for significance. Records, whether for the most objectives scored in a schedule year, the biggest number of aids a season, or the most lofty individual honors, address culminations that competitors try to prevail. The breaking of records turns into a demonstration of a competitor's persevering through effect, flexibility, and capacity to rise above the limits of the past. The measurable part of objectives and helps adds a quantitative aspect to the subjective brightness of on-field exhibitions. Objective scoring diagrams, help counts, and records become factual markers that add to a competitor's profile and heritage. In any case, underneath the numbers lies the story of commitment, flexibility, and the endless long periods of preparing and planning that finish in those snapshots of scoring objectives or making unequivocal helps. The factual records, while giving a depiction of a competitor's accomplishments, are improved by the narratives of assurance, difficulties survive, and the quest for greatness that goes with every objective and help.

The meaning of objectives, helps, and honors reaches out past the wearing field to the more extensive social effect of competitors. Objective scorers and playmakers become social symbols, their names inseparable from snapshots of donning splendor that enthrall crowds around the world. Honors add to a competitor's attractiveness, impacting underwriting arrangements, sponsorships, and the making of a brand that rises above the field of play. Competitors who reliably convey objectives and helps, combined with an assortment of honors, become donning legends as well as compelling figures with the capacity to shape cultural stories and move people in the future.

2. **Impact on the sport and community**

The effect of competitors on their particular games and networks addresses a powerful transaction between athletic ability, initiative, and social obligation. Past the field of play, competitors employ impact that stretches out a long ways past individual accomplishments, molding the way of life of their games and making a permanent imprint on the networks they address. The groundbreaking force of sports is encapsulated by the job competitors play in rousing, joining together, and driving positive change both inside the wearing domain and the more extensive society.

Competitors, as diplomats of their games, convey an obligation that rises above the quest for individual brilliance. Their exhibitions on the field become accounts that enthrall crowds, make enduring recollections, and add to the developing storylines of their games. Famous minutes, whether a game-dominating objective, a record-breaking accomplishment, or a presentation of excellent expertise, become characterizing parts in the aggregate memory of fans. Competitors who reliably convey such minutes become inseparable from the character of their games, adding to the rich embroidery of sports history.

The effect of competitors on the games they address is many times amplified during significant competitions and worldwide contests. Occasions like the Olympics, World Cups, and title finals become stages where competitors feature their abilities on the most stupendous scale. At these times, competitors rise above the limits of individual games and become images of public pride.

Their exhibitions raise the height of their games, draw in worldwide crowds, and cultivate a feeling of solidarity and fellowship among fans around the world. The reverberation of a competitor's effect is elevated when they lead their groups to triumph in lofty competitions, scratching their names in the archives of sports history.

Off the field, competitors become powerhouses who shape the way of life, standards, and upsides of their games. Their direct, both on and off the field, sets norms for sportsmanship, trustworthiness, and amazing skill. Competitors who encapsulate these characteristics become good examples, rousing more youthful ages to succeed in sports as well as to embrace standards of fair play, regard, and flexibility. The impact of competitors reaches out to the improvement of sports culture, where their decisions and activities add to the forming of accounts that characterize the ethos of their games.

The effect of competitors on their networks is a demonstration of the extraordinary force of sports as a bringing together power. Competitors, frequently well established in the places where they grew up or nations, become images of pride and motivation for neighborhood networks. They exemplify the goals of their networks, breaking boundaries, and beating difficulties to accomplish significance. Competitors who return to their networks, take part in altruism, and effectively add to neighborhood drives become impetuses for positive change, utilizing their leverage to resolve cultural issues and set out open doors for other people.

Generosity turns into a strong road through which competitors channel their effect toward significant social causes. The foundation of magnanimous establishments, commitment to local area outreach programs, and direct contribution in drives resolving issues like training, wellbeing, and civil rights exhibit the more extensive cultural effect of competitors. The assets and impact gathered through their wearing vocations become devices for having a substantial effect in the existences of those less lucky. Competitors who influence their foundation to reward their networks become brandishing symbols as well as ministers of social obligation.

The social effect of competitors reaches out to their job as supporters for civil rights and uniformity. In a period where sports are perceived as stages for cultural exchange, competitors progressively utilize their voices to resolve issues like racial disparity, orientation segregation, and fundamental shameful acts. Standing firm, partaking in developments, and participating in support become basic parts of a competitor's effect on society. Competitors who utilize their perceivability to support causes past games add to a more extensive story of social change, testing standards and cultivating inclusivity.

Initiative, both on and off the field, is a critical part of a competitor's effect. Skippers, group pioneers, and compelling figures inside sports associations become channels for molding group culture, encouraging solidarity, and motivating aggregate greatness.

The capacity to show others how its done, inspire partners, and explore difficulties with flexibility characterizes a competitor's authority influence. Past the bounds of sports, competitors frequently accept positions of authority in more extensive cultural settings, utilizing their leverage to advocate for positive change, guide more youthful ages, and add to the improvement of future pioneers.

The effect of competitors on networks is especially articulated in grassroots games and youth improvement programs. Competitors who effectively draw in with youthful trying gifts, act as guides, and add to the foundation of youth sports become draftsmen of the cutting edge's prosperity. Their association in training, instructive drives, and the arrangement of assets makes pathways for hopeful competitors to realize their true capacity. The mentorship and direction given by competitors in their networks become instrumental in molding the qualities, hard working attitude, and goals of people in the future.

The worldwide reach of sports enhances the effect of competitors, transforming them into worldwide powerhouses with the capacity to rise above geological and social limits. Competitors who contend on worldwide stages become social envoys, addressing their nations and sports on a worldwide scale. Their effect stretches out to a different crowd, cultivating associations, separating hindrances, and adding to a common worldwide encounter. The widespread language of sports turns into a course for building spans, encouraging comprehension, and advancing the upsides of collaboration and fair contest.

The effect of competitors on networks isn't safe to difficulties and debates. Occasions of competitor activism, conflicts with sports associations, or moral slips can mix discussions and shape public insights. The investigation that accompanies notoriety expects competitors to explore complex scenes, offsetting individual convictions with the assumptions for fans and partners. Competitors who explore these difficulties with straightforwardness, lowliness, and a guarantee to moral lead support the positive effect they can have on networks.

7.2 Leadership On and Off the Field

Initiative, both on and off the field, is a foundation of a competitor's effect and heritage. The characteristics that characterize powerful authority — motivation, strength, responsibility, and the capacity to join together and persuade a group — stretch out past the bounds of sports, molding the person and impact of competitors in more extensive cultural settings. Whether captaining a group in the intensity of rivalry or utilizing their foundation to support social causes, competitors who exemplify authority become chiefs of their games as well as persuasive figures equipped for guiding positive change.

On the field, the job of a pioneer is emphasizd in the pot of contest. Commanders, frequently distinguished as the emblematic tops of their groups, convey the obligation of directing their colleagues through the back and forth movements of a game. Authority in the wearing field requires a fragile harmony between essential discernment, persuasive ability, and the capacity to stay formed under tension. The chief's armband, worn proudly, turns into a noticeable image of power and obligation, mirroring the trust presented to the person to lead the group to progress.

The quintessence of on-field authority is exemplified in essential minutes — vital punishments, unequivocal plays, or game-evolving choices. Pioneers arise through individual splendor as well as by catalyzing aggregate exertion, encouraging solidarity, and imparting a common obligation to accomplishing group objectives. The capacity to mobilize colleagues during affliction, move certainty, and use wise judgment in basic points characterizes a competitor's authority influence on the field. The commander's job stretches out past being a talented player; it incorporates the ability to go about as an impetus for group union and achievement.

Off the field, administration takes on an alternate aspect as competitors influence their impact to impact positive change in the public eye. The perceivability and acknowledgment gathered through brandishing accomplishments make a stage that stretches out past the limits of the field. Competitors who embrace authority off the field become advocates for civil rights, equity, and local area advancement. Utilizing their voices to resolve cultural issues, they become influencers, testing standards, and moving others to take action accordingly.

Magnanimity turns into a strong articulation of off-field initiative, where competitors channel their assets and impact to help worthy missions. Laying out establishments, taking part in local area outreach programs, and effectively captivating in drives that address issues like training, medical services, and neediness show a promise to having an unmistakable effect. Competitors who show others how its done in rewarding their networks become donning legends as well as caring pioneers who figure out the more extensive obligations that accompany their impact.

Administration off the field is likewise obvious in the mentorship and direction that competitors give to more youthful ages. Perceiving the extraordinary force of sports in forming character, imparting discipline, and cultivating co-operation, competitors effectively participate in training, mentorship projects, and youth improvement drives. The guide mentee dynamic turns into a course for passing on specialized abilities as well as the immaterial characteristics of initiative, flexibility, and the significance of rewarding the local area.

The effect of off-field administration is amplified when competitors utilize their foundation to advocate for civil rights and balance. In a period where sports have become stages for cultural exchange, competitors progressively utilize their voices to resolve issues like racial disparity, orientation segregation, and foundational shameful acts.

Standing firm, partaking in developments, and participating in support become necessary parts of a competitor's administration influence off the field. Competitors who utilize their perceivability to support causes past games add to a more extensive story of social change, testing standards and cultivating inclusivity.

The advancement of administration in sports is reflected in the moving elements of group culture and hierarchical designs. Current games associations perceive the significance of enabling competitors as pioneers both on and off the field. Cooperative direction, open correspondence channels, and the consideration of competitors in essential conversations have become signs of moderate games administration. Competitors, thusly, play embraced parts that reach out past playing obligations, effectively taking part in group the executives, local area commitment, and adding to the improvement of a positive hierarchical culture.

The effect of administration isn't safe to difficulties and contentions. Competitors exploring the intricacies of distinction and public examination frequently end up in circumstances that test their authority characteristics. Moral predicaments, clashes with sports associations, and the strain of satisfying cultural hopes expect competitors to explore with versatility, modesty, and a pledge to moral lead. Pioneers who climate these difficulties with straightforwardness and trustworthiness support the positive effect they can have in their groups and networks.

The tradition of initiative is a story formed by individual accomplishments as well as by the persevering through influence on the way of life of sports and society. Pioneers who leave an enduring inheritance are recalled for their measurable achievements as well as for the qualities they typify, the positive change they impact, and the motivation they give to people in the future. Initiative, as a lived insight, turns into a powerful story that unfurls through a competitor's profession, developing with each test, win, and commitment to the more extensive local area.

1. **Captaincy and team dynamics**
   Captaincy in sports is a job of enormous importance, conveying the heaviness of authority, obligation, and the capacity to impact group elements. The commander, frequently perceived as the emblematic top of a group, assumes a critical part in molding the aggregate character, cultivating solidarity, and directing the group through the intricacies of rivalry. Past being a gifted player, a commander is a pioneer who explores the difficulties of the donning field, imparts a feeling of direction in the group, and turns into a nonentity for both achievement and strength.
   At the core of captaincy is the capacity to move and spur colleagues. A chief isn't simply a specialist or strategist; they are an impetus for positive energy and aggregate exertion. The motivational characteristics of a commander frequently manifest in urgent minutes, where a stirring discourse, a main as a visual cue execution, or a presentation of flexibility under tension can elevate the whole group.
   The chief's impact goes past individual commitments; it pervades the group's ethos, making a culture of conviction, assurance, and a common obligation to progress.
   Group elements, molded to a great extent by the skipper, are a fragile

equilibrium of characters, jobs, and cooperative endeavors. A commander's initiative style impacts how players collaborate, convey, and cooperate both on and off the field. Skippers who cultivate open correspondence, empower kinship, and construct a feeling of solidarity add to a good group climate. The skipper fills in as a key part, guaranteeing that singular gifts mix into a strong unit that is more prominent than the amount of its parts.

Key keenness is one more basic part of captaincy. In the intensity of contest, skippers should settle on split-subsequent options that can influence the result of a game. Whether it's a strategic change, a replacement, or an adjustment of approach, the skipper's capacity to peruse the game and settle on informed choices is instrumental. Vital reasoning reaches out past on-field elements to incorporate preparation, readiness, and versatility — characteristics that characterize a chief's part in controlling the group through the difficulties of a season or competition.

The skipper's job as a contact among players and instructing staff is vital to powerful group the executives. Chiefs act as courses for correspondence, conveying the mentor's systems, assumptions, and criticism to the players. Thus, they address the players' viewpoints, concerns, and experiences to the instructing staff. This powerful relationship requires a chief to have a profound comprehension of the game as well areas of strength for as abilities and the capacity to explore the intricacies of group elements.

A skipper's effect is many times amplified during times of misfortune. How a commander controls the group through testing times, rallies resolve, and ingrains versatility turns into a demonstration of their initiative. Misfortune can take different structures — series of failures, central member wounds, or outside pressures — and a chief's reaction establishes the vibe for how the group explores these difficulties. Skippers who stay made, motivate certainty, and show others how its done during difficult stretches become energizing focuses for the group's aggregate soul.

The job of a commander turns out to be especially articulated in individual games where the competitor is both player and pioneer. In tennis, for instance, a group commander in a Davis Cup or Took care of Cup setting should succeed on the court as well as give direction and inspiration to their colleagues. The independent idea of individual games adds an extra layer of liability to the chief's job, expecting them to offset individual execution with the initiative requests of directing a group.

The captaincy is many times a turning job in group activities, with various players taking on authority obligations in light of variables like insight, position, or explicit ranges of abilities. The most common way of choosing a skipper includes contemplations of on-field ability as well as characteristics like initiative, correspondence, and the capacity to move. Commanders, whether authoritatively named or arising as normal pioneers inside the group, lead of initiative, epitomizing the qualities and desires of the aggregate unit.

The imagery of the skipper's armband, shirt, or stately obligations highlights the chief's job as a nonentity for the group. These images address something other than power; they encapsulate a tradition of initiative that rises above individual players. Skippers frequently continue in the strides of venerated pioneers who have made a permanent imprint in the group's set of experiences. Wearing the chief's armband isn't simply an obligation; it's an association with a heredity of initiative, a noticeable connection to the practices and values that characterize the group.

The impact of a commander reaches out past the bounds of the battleground to the more extensive local area of fans and partners. Commanders become diplomats for the group, addressing its qualities, personality, and desires. The association between a skipper and the fanbase is frequently personal and emblematic, with the chief filling in as a conductor for the deepest desires of allies. The chief's effect is felt in triumphs as well as in the manner in which they exemplify the soul and ethos of the group, cultivating a feeling of satisfaction and having a place among fans.

Skippers are not invulnerable to difficulties and discussions. The investigation that accompanies initiative frequently includes exploring issues, for example, group questions, clashes with training staff, or advertising difficulties. How commanders handle these circumstances, showing flexibility, strategy, and a guarantee to group solidarity, shapes view of their initiative. Chiefs who explore difficulties with elegance and trustworthiness build up the positive effect they can have in group elements and the more extensive games local area.

2. **Philanthropy and community involvement**

Charity and local area association address strong elements of a competitor's effect, stretching out past the domains of rivalry to make positive change and add to the prosperity of society. Competitors, with their perceivability, impact, and assets, have the ability to be impetuses for social change, resolving major problems and making significant commitments to their networks. The crossing point of sports and magnanimity highlights the more extensive obligations that accompany acclaim and achievement, as competitors influence their foundation to impact positive change.

The humanitarian undertakings of competitors frequently come to fruition through the foundation of altruistic establishments or commitment with existing associations. These establishments act as vehicles for directing assets, both monetary and in-kind, toward drives that line up with the competitor's qualities and the necessities of the local area. The causes competitors decide to help are assorted, going from schooling and medical services to civil rights, ecological preservation, and destitution easing. By tending to fundamental difficulties, competitors add to the more extensive social texture, utilizing their foundation to intensify the effect of their altruistic endeavors.

Training arises as a point of convergence for some competitors took part in charity. The production of grant programs, financing for schools, and backing for instructive drives expect to break hindrances and give open doors to the people who might confront financial difficulties. Competitors perceive the groundbreaking force of schooling in shaping lives and utilize their leverage to advocate drives that encourage learning, ability improvement, and admittance to quality training. By putting resources into training, competitors add to a heritage that stretches out past the promptness of their vocations, making pathways for people in the future to succeed.

Medical care is another basic region where competitors make critical generous commitments. Drives might include subsidizing clinical exploration, supporting emergency clinics, or tending to explicit wellbeing challenges pervasive locally. Competitors, frequently keenly conscious about the significance of actual prosperity, utilize their foundation to advocate for wellbeing mindfulness, preventive measures, and admittance to clinical benefits. By putting resources into medical services, competitors add to the general prosperity of their networks, advancing better ways of life and tending to abberations in medical care access.

Civil rights and fairness have become conspicuous central focuses for competitors participated in altruism, especially lately. The worldwide perceivability of competitors gives a stage to pushing against racial imbalance, separation, and fundamental treacheries. Competitors utilize their voices, assets, and impact to help developments resolving these issues, frequently lining up with associations that work toward making an all the more and impartial society. Magnanimity in the domain of civil rights highlights the job of competitors as supporters for change, testing standards and adding to the more extensive story of cultural advancement.

Natural protection has likewise arisen as a huge area of concentration for competitors looking to have a beneficial outcome. Perceiving the ecological difficulties confronting the planet, competitors add to drives that advance supportability, preservation, and the assurance of normal assets. Whether through supporting eco-accommodating ventures, bringing issues to light about environmental change, or straightforwardly adding to preservation endeavors, competitors influence their impact to address the interconnected difficulties confronting the climate.

Local area association goes past monetary commitments and includes direct commitment with neighborhood networks. Competitors frequently partake in outreach programs, local area administration ventures, and occasions that carry them nearer to individuals they plan to affect. The active inclusion permits competitors to interface with the local area on an individual level, grasp its remarkable difficulties, and designer their charitable endeavors to address explicit requirements. This immediate commitment cultivates a feeling of kinship and fortitude, underscoring the competitor's obligation to being a functioning member in the improvement of the local area.

The effect of competitor charity reaches out to the people and networks straightforwardly contacted by their drives. Grants empower understudies to seek after advanced education, medical care drives give admittance to clinical benefits, and civil rights promotion adds to a more evenhanded society. The expanding influence of these commitments is felt in the prompt recipients as well as in the more extensive local area, making a good pattern of strengthening, motivation, and aggregate prosperity.

The job of competitor magnanimity in catastrophe alleviation and helpful guide is especially articulated during seasons of emergency. Catastrophic events, worldwide pandemics, and different crises require quick reactions, and competitors frequently move forward to offer help. Whether through monetary gifts, coordinating aid ventures, or utilizing their foundation to bring issues to light, competitors add to mitigating the prompt effects of fiascos and assisting networks with reconstructing. The dexterity and responsiveness of competitor generosity during emergencies feature the limit of sports figures to have a significant effect in the midst of dire need.

The perceivability of competitor generosity has expanded with the appearance of online entertainment and advanced stages. Competitors currently have direct channels to impart their charitable drives, share accounts of effect, and activate support from their fan bases. The capacity to interface with fans on an individual level, grandstand the effect of magnanimity, and energize more extensive cooperation has turned into an incredible asset for competitors focused on having a beneficial outcome. Online entertainment stages act as powerful center points for generous narrating, cultivating a feeling of local area commitment and rousing others to add to significant causes.

While competitor magnanimity is without a doubt a power for positive change, it isn't without its intricacies. The potential for influence is huge, however compelling charity requires cautious thought of local area needs, cooperation with experienced associations, and a supported obligation to long haul objectives. Competitors should explore the moral components of altruism, guaranteeing that their drives line up with veritable local area needs and add to manageable, evenhanded arrangements. The straightforwardness and responsibility of humanitarian endeavors are essential angles that competitors, as well known individuals, should maintain to keep up with the trust of their allies.

CHAPTER 8

The Peak of Glory

The apex of a competitor's profession is in many cases set apart by the summit of long periods of devotion, discipline, and steadfast obligation to their specialty. The pinnacle of greatness addresses the apex of accomplishment, where a competitor achieves the most elevated levels of progress, acknowledgment, and satisfaction in their picked sport. This pivotal stage isn't just an impression of individual ability yet in addition a demonstration of flexibility, penance, and the constant quest for greatness.

At the pinnacle of magnificence, competitors stand on the highest point of their accomplishments, having vanquished difficulties, outperformed achievements, and scratched their names in the records of brandishing history. The excursion to this peak is a story of steadiness, described by endless long stretches of preparing, beating misfortunes, and exploring the eccentric landscape of cutthroat games. The pinnacle isn't simply a transitory second yet the summit of a deep rooted mission for significance.

Accomplishing the pinnacle of brilliance frequently includes arriving at critical achievements, whether as record-breaking exhibitions, title triumphs, or individual honors. These achievements become permanent markers in the competitor's vocation, implying individual victories as well as commitments to the more extensive story of their game. Records broke and titles got become piece of the aggregate memory, woven into the texture of sports history.

Title triumphs stand apart as amazing accomplishments at the pinnacle of a competitor's vocation. The climax of a season-long excursion or a tiring competition, bringing home a title addresses a definitive approval of expertise, collaboration, and strength. The flavor of triumph isn't just an individual victory yet a common delight with colleagues, mentors, and fans who have been essential for the excursion. Title minutes become getting through recollections, carved in the hearts of the people who saw the pinnacle of magnificence.

Individual awards add to the radiance of the pinnacle, perceiving the competitor's excellent abilities and commitments to their game. Grants like MVP

(Most Important Player), Brilliant Boot, or Player of the Year become images of individual greatness. The pinnacle of brilliance is enhanced with the sparkling acknowledgment of friends, mentors, and the wearing local area, solidifying the competitor's heritage as truly outstanding in their field.

The Olympic Games, World Cups, and other worldwide rivalries give famous stages where competitors can arrive at the highest point of their vocations. Remaining on the platform, hung in gold, silver, or bronze, competitors relax in the greatness of addressing their nations on the world stage. The Olympic proverb "Citius, Altius, Fortius" (Quicker, Higher, More grounded) epitomizes the substance of the pinnacle of brilliance, where competitors endeavor to push the limits of human potential and accomplish accomplishments that resound past boundaries.

For some competitors, the pinnacle of brilliance isn't just about private accomplishment yet about moving others and leaving an enduring inheritance. The effect stretches out past the field of play, as competitors become good examples for yearning gifts, typifying the upsides of difficult work, persistence, and sportsmanship. The pinnacle turns into a guide of motivation, lighting the way for the up and coming age of competitors who really hope for arriving at comparable levels.

The pinnacle of brilliance is much of the time joined by a flood in open acknowledgment and deference. Competitors become easily recognized names, their appearances gracing magazine covers, announcements, and TV screens. The idolization of fans, the admiration of companions, and the affirmation from the worldwide brandishing local area make a powerful blend of notoriety and recognition. The competitor, when a wannabe with a fantasy, presently remains as a symbol at the peak of their game.

The monetary prizes that go with the pinnacle of greatness are significant, mirroring the attractiveness and business allure of effective competitors. Underwriting bargains, sponsorship agreements, and brand organizations become rewarding roads that open up as competitors climb to the pinnacle. The monetary bonus isn't simply an impression of brandishing ability yet in addition an acknowledgment of the competitor's impact and attractiveness on a worldwide scale.

The pinnacle of brilliance, in any case, isn't without any trace of difficulties and intricacies. The strain to keep up with maximized operation, the examination of public and media assumptions, and the requests of reliably conveying excellent outcomes can burden. Competitors at the pinnacle frequently wind up exploring a fragile harmony between the quest for greatness and the intrinsic weaknesses that accompany being at the center of attention.

The unavoidable section of time acquaints an extra aspect with the pinnacle of greatness. As competitors age, the actual requests of contest might cause significant damage, and keeping up with a similar degree of execution turns into an imposing test. The progress from the pinnacle of a profession to its dusk stage requires a recalibration of objectives, needs, and a smart thought of what comes straightaway.

For certain competitors, the pinnacle of brilliance is a transient stage, set apart by a particular second or a progression of victorious seasons. For other people, it addresses a supported time of strength, where greatness turns into a reliable sign of their professions. The life span of a competitor's pinnacle is impacted by elements like actual wellness, versatility, and the capacity to advance with the changing scene of their game.

Past the singular accomplishments, the pinnacle of brilliance frequently includes commitments to the more extensive games local area. Competitors take part in generosity, mentorship, and backing, utilizing their foundation to resolve cultural issues and have a constructive outcome. The progress from being a contender at the top to turning into a tutor and representative connotes a change in center from individual brilliance to a more extensive obligation to the prosperity of the donning biological system.

The story of the pinnacle of brilliance isn't bound to the competitor alone yet stretches out to the group, mentors, and the emotionally supportive network that assumed a crucial part in the excursion. Group elements, training ways of thinking, and the resolute help of loved ones structure a necessary piece of the account. The aggregate exertion that moves a competitor to the highest point is a demonstration of the collaboration of ability, direction, and a common obligation to progress.

The pinnacle of magnificence, in its embodiment, is a dynamic and developing story. It is a section in a competitor's story, a part set apart by wins, challenges, and the steady quest for greatness. A section resounds not just in the record books and prize cupboards however in the hearts of fans who share in the delight and festivity of the competitor's prosperity. The pinnacle is an impression of the human soul's ability to conquer obstructions, push limits, and arrive at phenomenal levels.

8.1 Culmination of Career

The summit of a competitor's profession addresses the end part of a wonderful excursion — an excursion set apart by wins, challenges, and a relentless obligation to the quest for greatness. An intelligent period exemplifies the ups and downs, the penances made, and the permanent effect the competitor has had on their game and the more extensive games local area. As the last whistle blows or the last race is run, the competitor changes from the pains of rivalry to a domain where the center movements from individual brilliance to a more extensive thought of inheritance, commitment, and the getting through engrave left on the brandishing scene.

One of the characterizing parts of the zenith of a profession is the choice to resign. Retirement is a groundbreaking decision that includes thought, self-evaluation, and a profound contemplation around one's actual capacities, mental strength, and by and large fulfillment with the excursion. For certain competitors, retirement is a choice made in their own particular manner, a cognizant decision to bow out at the pinnacle of their ability or on a high note. For other people, it could be provoked by elements like age, wounds, or a characteristic development of needs.

The retirement declaration, frequently conveyed with a blend of wistfulness and expectation for the following section, denotes the start of a change from the serious field to a more intelligent stage. It is a second while competitors, having accomplished what many can merely fantasize about, move back from the day to day afflictions of preparing, rivalry, and the unwavering quest for triumph. The declaration isn't simply an individual statement yet an aggregate affirmation from the wearing local area, fans, and friends that a part is coming to a nearby.

Pondering the excursion turns into a focal topic during the perfection of a profession. Competitors, presently managed the cost of the advantage of time away from the tireless requests of their game, return to the huge minutes, challenges survive, and the development of their abilities and outlook. The intelligent stage is a chance to see the value in the sum of the excursion — the early battles, the forward leaps, and the zenith of accomplishment. It is a chance to recognize the effect of mentors, colleagues, and the more extensive emotionally supportive network that assumed a urgent part in the competitor's direction.

The perfection of a vocation frequently includes a stylized goodbye — a second where the competitor is praised, regarded, and bid farewell by fans, colleagues, and the donning club. Goodbye matches, tribute occasions, and recognitions become impactful events that give conclusion to a section that has characterized a period. The close to home reverberation of these goodbyes highlights the significant association between the competitor and the local area that has mobilized behind them all through their profession.

Inheritance and commitment become the dominant focal point during the zenith of a profession. Competitors, aware of the effect they've had on their game and society, take part in exercises that add to the more extensive games local area. Numerous competitors channel their encounters and information into training, mentorship, or regulatory jobs, becoming stewards of the game and giving their insight to the future. The progress from being a contender to a guide is a groundbreaking stage that permits competitors to shape the fate of their game.

Altruism and local area inclusion likewise become basic parts of a competitor's post-retirement venture. Perceiving the social obligation that accompanies their foundation, resigned competitors frequently take part in drives that address cultural issues, support worthy missions, and have a constructive outcome past the domains of sports. The competitor turns into a diplomat for change, utilizing their impact to add to the prosperity of networks and advocating makes close their hearts.

The change to post-retirement life brings its own arrangement of difficulties. Competitors, acclimated with the design and routine of a cutthroat profession, explore the strange waters of an existence without everyday instructional meetings, serious installations, and the adrenaline of the game. The shift from an exceptionally controlled way of life to one that offers greater adaptability and decision requires a recalibration of schedules, objectives, and a redefinition of individual personality past the job of a functioning competitor.

For certain competitors, the summit of their serious profession denotes the start of new pursuits, frequently outside the domain of sports. Business, media adventures, and promotion become roads through which resigned competitors channel their energy and imagination. The abilities sharpened during their donning professions — discipline, strength, cooperation — act as important resources in different fields, permitting them to change consistently to new undertakings.

The actual cost of a cutthroat profession may likewise require contemplations for post-retirement wellbeing and prosperity. Competitors, receptive to the requests their bodies have persevered, frequently take part in post-vocation wellness regimens, medical services drives, and mindfulness crusades. The change to a more reasonable and wellbeing cognizant way of life turns into a need, guaranteeing that the actual tradition of the competitor's profession is one of life span and essentialness.

The media assumes a critical part in forming the story during the perfection of a profession. Competitors, presently resigned, frequently become sought-after pundits, experts, or media characters.

Their bits of knowledge, drawn from long periods of on-field insight, give a special point of view that improves the's comprehension crowd might interpret the game. The change to the media permits competitors to remain associated with the game they love, but from an alternate vantage point.

In the domain of sports, Corridor of Distinction enlistments stand as a demonstration of a competitor's enduring effect on their game. The summit of a vocation frequently tracks down its proper acknowledgment in the blessed corridors of brandishing everlasting status. Corridor of Notoriety services become snapshots of reflection, festivity, and an aggregate affirmation of the competitor's commitments to the game's rich embroidery.

The relational intricacy goes through a shift during the zenith of a vocation. Competitors, who might have spent huge periods from their families during the afflictions of contest, presently track down the chance to focus on and re-inforce familial bonds. The post-retirement stage turns into an opportunity to be available for life's achievements, appreciate quality time with friends and family, and embrace the job of a parent, accomplice, or kin with reestablished center.

The profound scene during the perfection of a profession is complex and nuanced. Competitors experience a range of feelings — appreciation for the help got, wistfulness for the minutes that characterized their excursion, and maybe a hint of despairing as they bid goodbye to the normal that has characterized a lot of their lives. The close to home goodbye, frequently joined by tears and grins, typifies the intricacy of changing from the natural to the unexplored world.

1. **Pinnacle moments and championships**

   Apex minutes and titles in the domain of sports are the crescendos that characterize a competitor's profession, denoting the peak of accomplishment and carving permanent recollections in the records of brandishing history. These minutes, whether on the fabulous phase of a title occasion or in the pot of individual greatness, address the zenith of tenacious devotion, steadfast responsibility, and the quest for greatness that characterizes the pith of sportsmanship.

   Titles, in different structures and across different games, stand as a definitive approval of a competitor's ability. The quest for a title frequently turns into a main impetus that shapes a competitor's excursion, directing their undertakings, and energizing the fire of rivalry. Whether it's the zenith of group activities like the Super Bowl in American football, the World Cup in soccer, or individual pursuits, for example, the Olympic gold decoration, titles epitomize the aggregate goals, dreams, and tries of competitors and groups.

   The meaning of titles reaches out past the conferral of titles and prizes. Bringing home a title is a demonstration of a group's union, strength, and capacity to perform under tension. It is the consequence of fastidious preparation, vital brightness, and the total effect of individual commitments that mix into an amicable aggregate exertion. Titles address the satisfaction of shared objectives and the finish of a season-long excursion set apart by ups and downs.

   For individual competitors, bringing home titles is much of the time the unparalleled accomplishment of a profession. The quest for individual brilliance, whether in tennis, golf, or olympic style sports, includes exploring a lone way where achievement or disappointment lays soundly on the shoulders of the competitor. Zenith minutes in individual games are in many cases solidified in notorious pictures — a runner crossing the end goal, a golf player sinking a last putt, or a tennis player lifting a Huge homerun prize. These pictures become getting through images of win, persistence, and the quest for greatness.

Zenith minutes and titles are not just about the substantial compensations of triumph. They exemplify the immaterial components that characterize sports — the adventure of contest, the fellowship manufactured through shared battles, and the close to home rollercoaster of celebration and misfortune. These minutes become piece of the aggregate memory of fans, imbued in the social texture of countries, and celebrated as achievements that rise above the limits of time.

The story of titles frequently includes famous contentions that lift the stakes and power of rivalry. Whether it's the celebrated fights between tennis legends like Federer and Nadal, the notable matchups in ball between Wizardry Johnson and Larry Bird, or the exemplary conflicts in soccer between everlasting opponents like Barcelona and Genuine Madrid, contentions enhance the show and meaning of titles. These experiences become the stuff of legend, making stories that resound for ages.

Titles are frequently connected with characterizing plays — those urgent minutes that solidify the result of a game or a season. The signal blender in ball, the latest possible moment objective in soccer, or the Leap of faith pass in football — this multitude of has become impact of the shared perspective, related in sports legend and replayed in feature reels. They are the minutes that change competitors into legends and hoist games into immortal works of art.

The excursion to a title is laden with difficulties, misfortunes, and snapshots of uncertainty. The capacity to conquer difficulty, return quickly from routs, and keep up with center despite extreme strain is a sign of title type competitors and groups. It is the versatility fashioned in the cauldron of rivalry that recognizes the people who stand on the platform from the individuals who miss the mark. Titles are not simply the finish of an excursion; they are the summation of the examples took in, the scars procured, and the development accomplished en route.

The mission for titles frequently includes actual ability as well as a psychological mettle that recognizes champions from their friends. The capacity to remain created in high-pressure circumstances, settle on split-subsequent options, and perform at top levels under the examination of a worldwide crowd separates champions. Mental flexibility turns into a strong weapon in the stockpile of competitors who try to arrive at the culmination of their separate games.

The close to home range of titles includes the delight of triumph and the misery of rout. The bittersweet tears satisfaction, the hugs of colleagues, and the delight of fans make a close to home embroidery that colors the parties. On the other hand, the grievousness of rout, the tears shed in shame, and the reflection that follows a misfortune add to the human show that unfurls on the terrific phase of titles. This profound wealth makes titles games as well as profoundly resounding human encounters. The tradition of titles reaches out a long ways past the quick brilliance existing apart from everything else. It turns into a part in the more extensive story of a competitor's profession, impacting the way that they are recollected and the way in which their commitments are esteemed throughout the entire existence of their game. Titles become the benchmarks against which competitors are estimated, their names perpetually scratched in the echelons of significance. The getting through tradition of titles isn't just about the prizes won however the motivation they give hoping for competitors, molding the fantasies of people in the future.

While titles address zenith minutes in a competitor's profession, the quest for significance frequently includes a ceaseless pattern of laying out new objectives, pushing limits, and looking for new difficulties. For competitors and groups with a title outlook, bringing home one championship is many times a preface to the yearn for more. The greats, driven by a voracious craving for greatness, end up attracted to new difficulties, anxious to add more parts to their heritage.

The effect of titles reaches out past the limits of the games field to impact more extensive cultural stories. Public pride, local area character, and social importance are frequently interwoven with the outcome of sports groups on the worldwide stage. Titles become events for aggregate festival, joining different networks in shared happiness and making enduring recollections that rise above the domain of sports.

2. **International recognition and awards**

Worldwide acknowledgment and grants comprise a renowned element of a competitor's profession, representing individual greatness as well as the affirmation of their commitments on a worldwide stage.

These honors act as markers of accomplishment, mirroring the competitor's effect on their game, their ability to rise above public limits, and their remaining among the world's tip top. The excursion to worldwide acknowledgment is frequently set apart by achievements, notorious exhibitions, and the nonstop quest for greatness that pushes competitors into the worldwide spotlight.

At the core of global acknowledgment is the affirmation of a competitor's uncommon expertise, ability, and effect on their particular game. Whether in group activities like soccer, b-ball, or individual pursuits like tennis or games, global acknowledgment hoists a competitor past the limits of territorial or public approval. It is a demonstration of their capacity to contend and succeed at the most significant levels, contending with the best from around the world.

One of the essential roads through which global acknowledgment is presented is through renowned honors. Praises like the Ballon d'Or in soccer, the

Laureus World Games Grants, and the ESPY Grants perceive competitors for their remarkable accomplishments, sportsmanship, and commitments to the worldwide wearing scene. These honors functions act as sparkling events that unite the's who of the donning scene, praising greatness and giving a stage to competitors to be recognized on a worldwide scale.

The meaning of worldwide acknowledgment stretches out past the singular competitor to the more extensive setting of sports discretion and social trade. Competitors become ministers for their nations, encapsulating the qualities, soul, and strength of their individual countries. The worldwide stage turns into a material on which competitors address themselves as well as their societies, characters, and the aggregate desires of their kinsmen. Worldwide acknowledgment turns into an extension that interfaces different networks through a common love for sports.

The rules for worldwide acknowledgment frequently go past on-field execution to envelop characteristics like sportsmanship, administration, and commitments to social causes. Competitors who utilize their foundation to advocate for civil rights, fairness, or participate in generosity improve their remaining in the worldwide games local area. Worldwide acknowledgment, in such cases, turns into an impression of a competitor's all encompassing effect, recognizing their job as forces to be reckoned with and specialists of positive change.

In group activities, addressing one's country in worldwide rivalries conveys an extraordinary reverberation. Contending in occasions like the FIFA World Cup, the Olympic Games, or the Rugby World Cup gives competitors an open door to feature their abilities on the most fabulous stage. Outcome in these competitions brings individual magnificence as well as raises the competitor to a status of public valor. Global acknowledgment, in this unique circumstance, is entwined with the aggregate pride of a country, as competitors become images of solidarity, versatility, and public character.

The renown of worldwide honors is enhanced by the worldwide investigation and rivalry they involve. The Ballon d'Or, for example, isn't simply an acknowledgment of the best player in a particular association however a proportion of greatness against the world's top gifts. The quest for these honors turns into a main thrust that urges competitors to reliably convey excellent exhibitions, no matter what the degree of contest they face. The worldwide benchmark recognizes the genuinely extraordinary from the simply exceptional.

The media assumes a critical part in forming worldwide acknowledgment. Competitors who catch the creative mind of worldwide crowds through their accomplishments on the field, magnetic characters, or convincing accounts are bound to get global recognition. The force of media, including online entertainment, enhances the compass of competitors past public boundaries, transforming them into worldwide symbols with fan bases crossing mainlands. The cooperative connection among competitors and the media adds to the story of global acknowledgment, making a pattern of perceivability, recognition, and impact.

Cooperation in worldwide contests and associations is a vital road for competitors to earn worldwide acknowledgment. Contending with top abilities from assorted foundations moves competitors to hoist their exhibition as well as opens them to various styles of play, procedures, and ways to deal with the game. The experience acquired in worldwide contests turns into a significant resource, improving a competitor's range of abilities and upgrading their versatility to various playing conditions.

The worldwide idea of sports fits a feeling of all inclusiveness and inclusivity. Competitors who rise above semantic, social, and geological hindrances to interface with a worldwide crowd frequently wind up at the very front of global acknowledgment. The capacity to convey and resound with fans from various corners of the world adds an additional layer of appeal to a competitor's persona, laying out them as ministers for the game on a global scale.

Worldwide acknowledgment isn't restricted to laid out competitors alone. Arising abilities who burst onto the scene with awesome exhibitions frequently end up slung into the worldwide spotlight. The quick spread of data in the computerized age permits these rising stars to earn global respect quickly, with fans, savants, and individual competitors paying heed to their true capacity. Global honors for youthful abilities, for example, the FIFA U-20 World Cup Brilliant Ball or the Laureus World Leap forward of the Year, act as stages to praise the commitment of the future.

The social effect of worldwide acknowledgment is obvious, rising above the limits of sports to impact mainstream society. Competitors who accomplish worldwide recognition become social symbols, their impact stretching out to domains past the battleground. The design business, supports, and coordinated efforts with craftsmen and artists are roads through which competitors add to forming worldwide patterns and social discussions. Worldwide acknowledgment turns into a course for competitors to make a permanent imprint in sports as well as in the more extensive social climate.

While global acknowledgment brings awards and recognition, it likewise puts competitors under extreme examination. The strain to reliably perform at the most significant level, the assumptions for fans and supporters, and the difficulties of adjusting individual and expert requests are inborn to the worldwide stage. Competitors who explore these tensions with elegance, flexibility, and legitimacy improve their global acknowledgment as well as develop an enduring inheritance as good examples.

8.2 Passing the Torch

"Passing the Light" with regards to sports is a strong and extraordinary second that typifies the progress of initiative, expertise, and inheritance starting with one age of competitors then onto the next. It addresses a continuum in the rich embroidery of sports history, where prepared veterans, having cut their names in the chronicles of significance, hand over the obligation and heritage to the arising gifts anxious to do something worth remembering. This emblematic exchange is weighed down with importance, connoting a top-down restructuring as well as the ceaselessness of the brandishing soul and the immortal quest for greatness.

At the core of "Passing the Light" lies the intergenerational discourse between experienced competitors and their replacements. This move isn't just about the actual passing of administration yet in addition includes the trading of information, shrewdness, and the significant illustrations earned from long periods of contest. The veterans become tutors, granting the subtleties of their specialty, the psychological strength required, and the systems that have moved them to progress. In doing as such, they establish the groundwork for the development and improvement of the arising gifts.

The imagery of "Passing the Light" frequently appears in conventional functions, emblematic signals, or cooperative endeavors among laid out and rising competitors. In group activities, it could include the active skipper giving over the chief's armband to the picked replacement. In individual games, it very well may be a resigning champion recognizing the arising star as the one ready to convey the heritage forward. These services become soul changing experiences, denoting the congruity of greatness and the affirmation of the obligations that accompany it.

The idea of "Passing the Light" is well established in the coach mentee relationship. Laid out competitors, having explored the ups and downs of their vocations, grasp the meaning of mentorship in encouraging the future. The tutor fills in as a directing power, offering bits of knowledge into the afflictions of contest, sharing individual encounters, and offering close to home help. This mentorship rises above the specialized parts of the game, incorporating the qualities, morals, and initiative characteristics that characterize a genuine athlete.

In the domain of group activities, the most common way of "Passing the Light" frequently includes a purposeful and key methodology by mentors and group the board. Distinguishing arising gifts, prepping them through mentorship programs, and continuously coordinating them into the group texture guarantees a consistent change. This purposeful passing of liabilities permits the approaching players to gain from the carefully prepared veterans, ingest the group culture, and progressively accept positions of authority as they advance.

The imagery of the actual light conveys verifiable and social undertones. In the Olympic Games, the lighting of the Olympic light during the initial service is a custom that represents coherence, solidarity, and the persevering through soul of contest. The light is lit by the last sprinter of the light hand-off, frequently a promising youthful competitor, who then passes it to the main competitor of the host country. This stylized demonstration reverberates with the more extensive subject of "Passing the Light," meaning the ceaseless fire of sportsmanship and the continuous tradition of athletic accomplishment.

A basic part of "Passing the Light" is the acknowledgment and preparation of the arising gifts to bear the obligations that accompany acquiring the heritage. This change requires expertise and ability as well as a significant comprehension of the qualities implanted in the brandishing venture. The torchbearers of the cutting edge should be outfitted with specialized ability as well as with the versatility, sportsmanship, and obligation to the standards of fair play that characterize the pith of sports.

The elements of "Passing the Light" are not restricted to the battleground alone yet stretch out to the more extensive games environment. Mentors, chairmen, and even fans assume critical parts in working with this change. Mentors, drawing from their own encounters, guide youthful gifts in improving their abilities, imparting discipline, and sustaining an outlook helpful for progress. Chairmen guarantee that designs are set up to recognize, support, and advance arising abilities, encouraging a climate where the light can be consistently passed.

Fans, the soul of sports, additionally add to the account of "Passing the Light." They witness the development of competitors, put genuinely in their excursions, and embrace the novices as they step into the shoes of their ancestors. The light passes between competitors as well as starting with one age of fans then onto the next, making a continuum of energy, reliability, and shared encounters that characterize the social meaning of sports.

The figurative passing of the light is many times joined by a feeling of wistfulness as fans observer the flight of dearest veterans. This wistfulness, nonetheless, is tempered by the energy and expectation of seeing new abilities leave on their own excursions. The close to home speculation fans have in competitors rises above the individual, turning into an aggregate festival of the game's heritage and the persevering through soul of rivalry.

A notorious part of "Passing the Light" is seen in the domain of individual accomplishments and records. As veteran record-holders resign or move toward the sundown of their professions, arising gifts arise to challenge and out-perform the benchmarks set by their ancestors. The breaking of records turns into an emblematic passing of the light, implying the development of the game and the never-ending journey for new levels of greatness.

The idea of "Passing the Light" isn't restricted to retirement situations alone; it likewise happens inside the course of a competitor's profession. In group activities, the shift of influential positions from prepared players to more youthful partners is a steady cycle. As players mature, gain insight, and feature administration characteristics, the light of captaincy or on-field initiative is frequently passed flawlessly, guaranteeing the group's progression and versatility to evolving elements.

In the more extensive setting of cultural accounts, "Passing the Light" in sports reflects more extensive subjects of progression, recharging, and the recurrent idea of life. It reflects the advances saw in different features of society, where the insight of the more established age joins with the energy and development of the more youthful age to drive progress. The imagery of the light rises above sports, turning into a widespread representation for the interminability of human undertakings.

The effect of "Passing the Light" stretches out past the bounds of the wearing field. Competitors who embrace this change become players as well as stewards of the game. They add to the forming of the future, motivating youthful gifts to think beyond practical boundaries, really buckle down, and maintain the upsides of sportsmanship. The torchbearers, thusly, convey the obligation not exclusively to succeed in their game yet in addition to add to its development, maintainability, and positive effect on society.

1. **Mentoring the next generation**

   Coaching the cutting edge in sports is a significant and fundamental part of the athletic excursion, encapsulating the exchange of information, experience, and values from prepared veterans to arising gifts. This mentorship dynamic reaches out past the bounds of the battleground, incorporating a comprehensive way to deal with supporting the development, character, and capability of youthful competitors. In the domain of sports, tutoring turns into an extraordinary cycle that shapes individual professions as well as adds to the more extensive culture of cooperation, strength, and the quest for greatness.

   At its center, coaching is a harmonious relationship that spans the generational hole, interfacing prepared competitors with the people who are simply leaving on their excursion. The tutor, frequently a refined and experienced figure in the game, assumes the job of an aide, friend, and wellspring of shrewdness for the mentee.

   This relationship goes past the specialized parts of the game, digging into the subtleties of mental versatility, initiative, and the immaterial characteristics that characterize a fruitful competitor.

   Coaching in sports is in many cases formalized through mentorship programs, particularly in proficient associations and foundations. These projects pair experienced competitors with more youthful partners, making organized systems for direction, backing, and expertise improvement. In such projects, the guide turns into a wellspring of motivation, offering experiences into the complexities of the game, sharing individual stories, and giving a guide to exploring the difficulties of a serious vocation.

The mentorship interaction is certainly not a one-size-fits-all approach however a customized and customized venture that perceives the remarkable requirements, qualities, and goals of each mentee. Guides concentrate on understanding the singular elements of their mentees — their playing style, mental cosmetics, and life outside the game. This customized approach empowers tutors to give designated direction that heads past the nonexclusive exhortation, cultivating a feeling of trust and shared understanding.

One of the crucial jobs of coaches in sports is the transmission of specialized ability. The guide, having leveled up their abilities through long stretches of involvement, turns into a significant asset for refining the specialized parts of the game. Whether it's culminating a specific method, grasping strategic subtleties, or fostering an essential mentality, the guide bestows an abundance of information that speeds up the mentee's expectation to learn and adapt.

Notwithstanding, coaching in sports rises above the Xs and operating system of the game; it envelops the intangibles that characterize a fruitful competitor. Tutors ingrain a feeling of discipline, hard working attitude, and impressive skill that goes past the field of play. They stress the significance of predictable exertion, scrupulousness, and the strength expected to climate the ups and downs of a games profession. These illustrations stretch out past the domain of sports, forming the person and attitude of the mentee in all aspects of life.

Tutoring likewise fills in as a conductor for the transmission of social and group values. In group activities, particularly, tutors assume a vital part in adjusting youthful competitors to the group culture, encouraging fellowship, and imparting a feeling of aggregate liability. The coach turns into a living encapsulation of the group's ethos, and through their activities, they set the principles for incredible skill, cooperation, and shared regard that structure the bedrock of effective group elements.

The daily reassurance given by coaches couldn't possibly be more significant. The tutor, having explored the close to home rollercoaster of a games vocation, turns into a mainstay of help during testing times. They offer a thoughtful ear, share their own encounters of conquering mishaps, and give viewpoint during snapshots of self-question. This profound direction is priceless, helping mentees explore the inborn vulnerabilities and tensions that accompany a lifelong in sports.

Past the prompt donning setting, tutors frequently become wellsprings of life counsel. They share bits of knowledge on dealing with the requests of acclaim, taking care of media examination, and adjusting individual and expert responsibilities. The mentorship relationship stretches out into regions, for example, monetary education, vocation arranging, and self-awareness, adding to the all encompassing development and prosperity of the mentee.

The mentorship cycle in sports isn't restricted to the playing years alone yet frequently reaches out into post-retirement stages. Numerous competitors, having profited from mentorship during their playing professions, keep on filling in as guides in different limits in the wake of resigning from dynamic rivalry. This recurrent nature of mentorship makes a tradition of information move that traverses ages, adding to the ceaselessness of wearing greatness.

In group activities, skippers frequently expect a true job as guides. The commander, normally an accomplished and regarded individual from the group, leads on the field as well as guides and tutors more youthful players. They act as a conductor between the training staff and the players, offering bits of knowledge into group elements, methodologies, and the unwritten principles of the game. The chief's job as a coach turns out to be especially significant during times of change or while coordinating new players into the group.

The mentorship dynamic additionally tracks down articulation in training connections. Mentors, frequently previous competitors themselves, carry a tutoring aspect to their jobs. They grasp the mind of competitors, understand their difficulties, and give an organized climate to development. In training, the coach fills in as a planner, inspiration, and figure of power, directing competitors through the formative phases of their vocations.

Tutoring in sports significantly affects variety and consideration. Prepared competitors who have pioneered trails in their particular games frequently act as tutors to those breaking hindrances or entering spaces generally overwhelmed by specific socioeconomics. This mentorship cultivates a feeling of having a place, gives good examples to hopeful competitors from different foundations, and adds to the destroying of fundamental boundaries inside the wearing scene.

The coach mentee relationship isn't one-layered; it develops over the long haul and adjusts to the changing requirements of the mentee. As the mentee gains insight, the mentorship dynamic might move from a more mandate way to deal with one described by shared bits of knowledge, coordinated effort, and common learning. This advancement mirrors the normal movement of the mentee's development and improvement inside the game.

The effect of coaching reaches out to the more extensive games local area. Competitors who have profited from mentorship frequently become advocates for organized mentorship programs inside sports associations and organizations. They perceive the potential for mentorship to add to the general wellbeing and supportability of sports environments, encouraging a culture of mentorship that stretches out from grassroots levels to proficient associations.

2. **Shaping the future of the sport**

Molding the fate of a game is a dynamic and multi-layered try that includes the aggregate endeavors of competitors, managers, mentors, and devotees. It is a forward-looking obligation to development, inclusivity, and supportability, pointed toward guaranteeing the getting through importance and development of the game for a long time into the future. This course of forming what's to come goes past prompt successes and misfortunes; it includes vital preparation, visionary initiative, and a profound comprehension of the developing scene wherein the game exists.

A significant part of forming the eventual fate of a game is encouraging a culture of development. Embracing innovative headways, information examination, and sports science becomes basic to improve execution, alleviate wounds, and push the limits of human potential. This obligation to development isn't restricted to the tip top levels of the game yet pervades through all levels, from grassroots to proficient associations. Associations put resources into innovative work, team up with innovation accomplices, and influence information driven experiences to refine preparing techniques and advance competitor execution.

Inclusivity is one more foundation of molding the fate of a game. Separating obstructions and making pathways for different support cultivates a rich and dynamic games environment. Drives pointed toward expanding openness, particularly at the grassroots level, guarantee that the game turns into a widespread pursuit. This inclusivity reaches out past orientation, nationality, and financial status to embrace people with handicaps, giving versatile projects and offices that empower everybody to encounter the delight and advantages of sports.

Youth improvement turns into a point of convergence in molding the fate of a game. Laying out powerful youth projects, foundations, and improvement pathways is fundamental to distinguish and sustain ability since the beginning.

This interest in youth not just fills in as an ability pipeline for the game yet additionally adds to character improvement, imparting upsides of discipline, collaboration, and versatility. Youth commitment drives, including school organizations and local area outreach, make a grassroots development that frames the bedrock for the game's future.

Key organizations with instructive establishments assume a significant part in molding the fate of a game. By incorporating sports into the educational program, schools become hatcheries for ability improvement and all encompassing competitor training. This coordinated effort stretches out to grant programs, setting out open doors for hopeful competitors to simultaneously seek after their scholar and wearing desires. The collaboration among sports and training adds to the general balanced improvement of competitors, setting them up for a double vocation in sports and scholastics.

Putting resources into framework is a substantial approach to forming the eventual fate of a game. Best in class preparing offices, present day arenas, and local area sports buildings establish a climate helpful for elite execution preparing and observer commitment. Framework improvement stretches out past metropolitan habitats to include country regions, guaranteeing that ability is uncovered and supported independent of geological limitations. These offices likewise become centers for sports the travel industry, drawing in occasions and contests that hoist the game's profile on a worldwide scale.

In forming the fate of a game, overseeing bodies and heads assume a significant part. Key preparation, straightforward administration, and compelling authority are fundamental to control the game in the correct bearing. Embracing best practices in sports organization, including moral navigation, monetary manageability, and competitor government assistance, fabricates trust inside the donning local area and guarantees the game's life span. Administrative structures that offset serious uprightness with advancement encourage a climate where the game can develop while safeguarding its basic beliefs.

Internationalization is a vital component of molding the eventual fate of a game. Growing the worldwide impression of the game through global contests, associations, and organizations expands its fan base as well as advances social trade and coordinated effort. Vital collusions with worldwide games organizations, cross-line associations, and worldwide promoting drives add to the game's rise as a really worldwide peculiarity. This internationalization upgrades the game's flexibility and versatility in an interconnected world.

The mix of virtual entertainment and computerized stages is a contemporary basic in forming the fate of a game. Utilizing these channels intensifies the game's perceivability as well as encourages direct commitment with fans. Competitors become forces to be reckoned with, and the game turns into a way of life that rises above the limits of the battleground.

Computerized advancement reaches out to fan encounters, empowering vivid and intuitive cooperation, from augmented reality broadcasts to dream sports associations.

Manageability is an essential thought in molding the eventual fate of a game. Associations are progressively perceiving the significance of ecological obligation, moral obtaining, and local area commitment in their tasks. Green drives, squander decrease programs, and eco-accommodating occasion the executives add to the game's positive effect on the climate. In addition, local area outreach programs, pointed toward advancing wellbeing and prosperity through sports, adjust the game to more extensive cultural objectives.

The development of the fan experience is an essential part in molding the fate of a game. Past customary spectatorship, present day fans look for vivid and customized encounters. Expanded reality, computer generated reality, and intuitive fan zones change the manner in which crowds draw in with the game. Making a feeling of local area through devoted groups of followers, online gatherings, and get-togethers guarantees that the fan base turns into a functioning and vital piece of the game's biological system.

Ladies' cooperation and portrayal become focal contemplations in forming the eventual fate of a game. Advancing orientation value, equivalent open doors, and perceivability for female competitors add to an additional comprehensive and various games scene. Interest in ladies' associations, advancement projects, and promoting drives raises the profile of ladies' games and motivates the up and coming age of female competitors. The eventual fate of the game is characteristically attached to cultivating a climate where ability knows no orientation limits.

Embracing a worldwide outlook is significant in forming the fate of a game. Understanding and adjusting to the social subtleties of various locales guarantees that the game reverberates with different crowds. Fitting showcasing systems, occasion configurations, and commitment missions to suit territorial inclinations adds to the game's acknowledgment and prominence across differed socioeconomics. This worldwide methodology rises above geological boundaries, encouraging a feeling of solidarity among fans around the world.

Interest in sports science and sports medication arises as a critical consider molding the eventual fate of a game. Progressions in injury avoidance, recovery methods, and competitor prosperity add to drawn out and supportable vocations. Sports science improves execution as well as guarantees the life span of competitors, limiting the actual cost of extreme focus rivalry. Coordinating all encompassing competitor care into the game's system turns into a foundation of dependable and forward-looking games the board.

Advancing moral lead and fair play is essential to molding the fate of a game. Carrying out powerful enemy of doping measures, guaranteeing uprightness in directing, and resolving issues of debasement add to the game's validity and dependability. Competitors who epitomize the standards of fair play become representatives for the game, setting norms for sportsmanship and moral way of behaving. Moral administration shields the game's trustworthiness as well as draws in patrons, accomplices, and a worldwide crowd that values straightforwardness and responsibility.

CHAPTER 9

Conclusion

All in all, the excursion through the unpredictable embroidery of football, from its verifiable roots to the worldwide stage, offers an all encompassing perspective on the game's widespread allure, the introduction of desire, and the early motivations that shape the fates of yearning players. It takes us through the youth accounts of incredible players, their most memorable experiences with a football, and the fantasies that come to fruition on dusty jungle gyms and swarmed roads.

The account unfurls further as the players progress, joining neighborhood youth groups, exploring the underlying battles and wins, and confronting the difficulties that test their backbone. It investigates the ascent through the positions, from school and novice associations to conquering impediments and difficulties, with mentorship and direction assuming vital parts in the competitors' turn of events.

The competitors' process picks up speed as they enter the pot of contest, encountering the force of school and public competitions, and fashioning extreme contentions that become pivotal occasions in their vocations. Arising as champion players, they get the hit up to the public group, addressing their nations on the fabulous stage and encountering the strain, pride, and public magnificence that accompany it.

The change to the expert domain denotes a huge stage in the competitors' vocations, from making their club presentation to joining proficient groups, encountering the primary taste of tip top rivalry, and laying out a presence in the wildly cutthroat scene. Ability advancement and sharpening mastery become foremost, as does earning respect on the public stage.

Preliminaries and wins, high-stakes matches, and title pursuits become the characterizing sections of their expert process. The competitors face impressive rivals and difficulty, encountering self-awareness on and off the field. Adjusting popularity, family, and individual life turns into a fragile yet fundamental part of their vocations.

As the competitors rise to the pinnacle of their vocations, they make a permanent imprint, with regards to record-breaking accomplishments as well as in their effect on the game and the local area. Their initiative on and off the field turns into a wellspring of motivation, and they explore the intricacies of captaincy and group elements with beauty. Participating in charity and local area inclusion, they add to the improvement of society, leaving a heritage that stretches out past their playing days.

The zenith of their vocations turns into an impression of long periods of devotion, penance, and immovable obligation to the game they love. Apex minutes and titles become the delegated gems in their renowned lifetimes, as global acknowledgment and grants cement their status as legends of the game.

As they pass the light to the future, tutoring turns into a basic part of forming the fate of the game. The competitors, presently stewards of the game, put resources into youth advancement, embrace inclusivity, and add to the more extensive games biological system. They become instrumental in directing yearning competitors, cultivating a culture of development, and guaranteeing the manageability and worldwide allure of the game.

In this excursion through the universe of football, from grassroots to worldwide conspicuousness, the competitors' accounts rise above the limits of the actual game. They become stories of versatility, assurance, and the quest for greatness. Their encounters reverberate with fans, moving the up and coming age of players and cultivating a feeling of local area that rises above topographical, social, and generational partitions.

As we consider this excursion, we witness the advancement of character and administration, the effect on the game and the local area, and the persevering through heritage that these competitors abandon. Their preliminaries and wins, both on and off the field, portray the groundbreaking force of sports and the dauntless soul that impels competitors to significance.

In the more extensive setting of the brandishing scene, these accounts highlight the general allure of football. A game goes past the limits of the battleground, making a common language that joins individuals from different foundations. The energy, fellowship, and aggregate festival that football induces make it a social peculiarity that rises above borders and turns into a wellspring of euphoria, motivation, and solidarity.

In the stupendous embroidery of football, every player's process is a string that winds around together the rich story of the game's set of experiences. From the dusty roads where dreams are brought into the world to the excellent arenas where heritages are carved in magnificence, football stays a demonstration of the human soul's vast potential and the persevering through force of a game that catches the hearts and minds of millions all over the planet.

9.1 Reflection on the Journey

As we set out on an intelligent excursion through the sweeping scene of football, from its grassroots starting points to the worldwide stage, it becomes obvious that the game is in excess of a game — a significant human encounter rises above geological limits, social contrasts, and generational movements. This review investigation permits us to dig into the complex woven artwork of football, unwinding the widespread allure, the introduction of aspiration, and the early motivations that shape the predeterminations of yearning players.

The excursion unfurls like an enamoring story, acquainting us with the youth accounts of unbelievable players whose underlying experiences with a football occurred on dusty jungle gyms and swarmed roads. These accounts resound with a common feeling of sentimentality, inspiring recollections of blameless-ness, enthusiasm, and the sheer delight of pursuing a fantasy. The fantasies that come to fruition in these early stages become the fuel that pushes people into a reality where desire exceeds all logical limitations.

The stories of these competitors take us through the maze of their child-hood, where joining neighborhood youth groups turns into a soul changing experience. It is here that the seeds of commitment are planted, and the under-lying battles and wins become the structure blocks of character and strength. The nearby youth groups, frequently the hatcheries of ability, act as cauldrons where crude potential is shaped into expertise, cooperation is sharpened, and the kinship fashioned on the pitch turns into a persevering through bond.

Exploring the way from nearby youth groups to more extensive stages includes conquering obstructions and mishaps — an excursion set apart by ups and downs that test the strength of trying players. Nonetheless, it is during these difficult minutes that mentorship and direction arise as priceless assets. Mentors, prepared players, and compelling figures become reference points of help, offering specialized experiences as well as the insight gathered from their own excursions.

The movement through school and novice associations turns into a urgent stage in the competitors' development. These associations act as demonstrat-ing grounds, where gifts are displayed, contentions escalate, and the power of rivalry arrives at new levels. School and novice associations additionally estab-lish the groundwork for the's comprehension competitors might interpret the more extensive elements of the game, showing them the significance of disci-pline, sportsmanship, and the unwavering quest for greatness.

First experiences with a football, frequently carved in lifelong recollections, take on a significant importance as we investigate the competitors' initial mo-tivations. These experiences become the impetuses for dreams, getting under way an excursion that rises above the limits of topography and culture. Dreams come to fruition in the personalities of youthful players, powered by the rever-berations of cheers from swarmed arenas and the quiet assurance to make a permanent imprint on the game they love.

As the competitors progress through their excursions, joining neighborhood youth groups and exploring the underlying battles, their fantasies become the dominant focal point. These fantasies become signals of desire, pushing them forward despite affliction and forming their ways of life as people and as competitors. The introduction of desire isn't simply an individual mission for brilliance; an aggregate pursuit interlaces with the more extensive story of football as a social peculiarity.

The general allure of football lies in its capacity to resound with individuals from varying backgrounds. A game rises above boundaries, dialects, and social hindrances, making a common language that joins millions all over the planet. The accounts of these competitors mirror the worldwide embroidered artwork of football, where different stories merge on the shared conviction of the pitch. The social extravagance implanted in the game turns into a wellspring of pride, character, and a common feeling of having a place for fans around the world.

The excursion stretches out past individual goals, addressing the aggregate encounters of experience growing up stories that reflect the general topics of companionship, versatility, and the quest for dreams.

The competitors' memories of their most memorable experiences with a football reverberation the aggregate recollections of fans who, sooner or later in their lives, kicked a ball in a rear entryway or joined companions in an improvised game on a fix of grass. These common encounters structure the connective tissue that ties the worldwide football local area.

Joining nearby youth groups turns into a urgent section in the competitors' accounts, set apart by the manufacturing of bonds that go past the bounds of the pitch. The brotherhood created inside these groups turns into a demonstration of the force of game in cultivating connections, imparting values, and sustaining a feeling of having a place. The nearby youth groups become microcosms of the more extensive football culture, where fellowships are framed, illustrations are learned, and the aggregate quest for progress turns into a common undertaking.

The excursion through the underlying battles and wins is a story that resounds generally. It is a demonstration of the human soul's versatility, the ability to beat difficulties, and the faithful obligation to a fantasy. The battles become transitional experiences, molding the competitors' characters and invigorating their assurance. The victories, whether large or little, become markers of progress, building up the conviction that each misfortune is a venturing stone toward more noteworthy accomplishments.

The scene of school and novice associations turns into a material where the competitors paint their accounts with enthusiasm, expertise, and an enduring longing to leave an imprint. These associations are something other than fields for rivalry; they are pots where ability is tried, contentions are produced, and the substance of the game is refined into snapshots of splendor.

The competitors' excursions through these associations become microcosms of the more extensive football story, where the quest for greatness is a common desire.

The mentorship and direction got during the excursion become vital parts in the competitors' stories. Mentors, prepared players, and powerful figures become coaches, giving specialized information as well as the intangibles that characterize genuine sportsmanship. These coaches act as directing lights, offering bits of knowledge drawn from their own encounters and becoming priceless wellsprings of help during the competitors' early stages.

The section from school and beginner associations to the cauldron of rivalry denotes a critical point in the competitors' excursions. The power of school and public competitions turns into the scenery for the competitors' proceeded with development, where the stakes are higher, and the opposition is more imposing. The competitors address their establishments and countries as well as convey the heaviness of aggregate assumptions and the quest for public magnificence.

The development as champion players intensifies the competitors' effect on the game and the local area. Their processes become entwined with the more extensive account of football, where individual accomplishments add to the game's aggregate inheritance. The hit up to the public group turns into a zenith second, addressing individual accomplishment as well as an acknowledgment of the competitors' commitments to the game on a public scale.

The change to the expert domain turns into an extraordinary stage, set apart by huge achievements, for example, making club makes a big appearance and joining proficient groups. The competitors' most memorable taste of tip top rivalry impels them into a domain where the edges among progress and dis-appointment are razor-dainty. Laying out a presence in this furiously serious scene requires expertise as well as mental guts, versatility, and a persevering hard working attitude.

The competitors' accounts, as they progress through the preliminaries and wins of their expert professions, become stories of self-improvement on and off the field. Adjusting popularity, family, and individual life turns into a sensitive shuffling act that mirrors the intricacies of current games. The competitors become players as well as people of note, exploring the requests of superstar while endeavoring to keep a feeling of validness and groundedness.

9.2 Looking back on a legendary career

As we turn our look towards the distinguished lifetimes of football legends, there is a significant feeling of wonder and deference for the permanent im-print they have left on the game. Thinking back on an unbelievable profession isn't simply a review work out; it is an excursion through the records of foot-ball history, a story woven with the strings of wins, challenges, and the resolute obligation to greatness.

The reflection on an unbelievable profession frequently starts with the early stages, where the seeds of energy and ability were planted on the modest grounds of young life. It is in these early years that the yearning footballers, presently venerated as legends, made their most memorable strides with a ball, envisioned their most memorable dreams, and lighted the flash that would fuel a long period of commitment to the delightful game.

The excursion through nearby youth groups and beginner associations turns into a pot of character, a proving ground where crude ability is refined, and kinship with individual players is manufactured. The legends, presently prepared competitors, think back about the guides and mentors who assumed significant parts in molding their abilities and imparting the qualities that would characterize their professions. The reverberations of roots for from allies those humble contributes still resonate their recollections, a demonstration of the grassroots beginnings that anchor even the most celebrated vocations.

The early battles and wins, carved in the records of their childhood, become sections of versatility and assurance. These legends review the snapshots of difficulty, the misfortunes that might have dissuaded a less steadfast soul, and the victories that noticeable the start of their climb. Thinking back, they recognize that it was the triumphs as well as the examples learned in shame that became necessary to their development as competitors and people.

The change from nearby associations to more extensive stages, including school and beginner rivalries, fills in as a scaffold between the crude ability of youth and the more complex requests of expert football. As these legends think back about those early stages, they perceive the significance of these venturing stones, where they leveled up their abilities, fostered a strategic keenness, and acquired openness to a more extensive crowd.

Mentorship and direction arise as repeating subjects in the reflections on unbelievable professions. Mentors and persuasive figures who perceived and supported their possible become the unrecognized yet truly great individuals in the account. The direction got during those early years molded their playing styles as well as imparted a mentality of ceaseless improvement and a pledge to the ethos of the game.

The excursion to school and public competitions adds a layer of intricacy to the reflections. It is on these stages that the legends addressed their schools or countries as well as defied the elevated assumptions and tensions that accompany contending at a more significant level. The recollections of school greatness and public call-ups summon a feeling of satisfaction, highlighting the effect these legends had on the bigger football scene.

The rise as champion players, decorated with honors and grants, denotes a defining moment in their professions. These legends, presently venerated as among the best on the planet, submissively think back on the minutes that characterized their ascent to noticeable quality. The main taste of world class rivalry, the significant matches, and the titles won become the structure blocks of their amazing status. Every objective scored, each help gave, and every prize lifted is a demonstration of their expertise, commitment, and the capacity to perform under tension.

As the reflections dig into the expert domain, the legends describe the difficulties looked in making club makes a big appearance and joining proficient groups. The change from hopeful youth to proficient competitor is a groundbreaking excursion set apart by better standards, extreme rivalry, and the acknowledgment that accomplishment at the most significant level requires ability as well as mental backbone and versatility.

Adjusting notoriety, family, and individual life arises as a repetitive topic in the stories of unbelievable professions. The requests of the spotlight, the tensions of being an individual of note, and the difficulties of keeping a feeling of predictability become basic parts of their accounts. The legends share experiences into the fragile harmony they looked to strike between their expert and individual lives, recognizing the penances made in quest for significance.

The pot of rivalry, where the legends confronted impressive adversaries and difficulty, turns into a focal topic in their appearance. The high-stakes coordinates, the extreme competitions, and the quest for titles characterize this period of their vocations. They think back on the snapshots of win that scratched their names in football history, recognizing the aggregate endeavors of colleagues, mentors, and fans that added to those triumphs.

The change to worldwide contest, addressing their nations on the fantastic stage, is an unparalleled accomplishment in the impressions of these legends. The strain, pride, and public greatness become characterizing components of their excursions. The distinction of wearing the public tones, driving their groups, and adding to the aggregate story of public achievement is a wellspring of monstrous pride and an esteemed part in their celebrated vocations.

As they ponder the zenith minutes and titles, the legends recognize the significant effect these encounters had on their inheritances. The recollections of lifting renowned prizes, commending with colleagues and fans, and carving their names in the record books become immortal engravings of their commitments to the game. Every title won isn't simply an individual accomplishment however a demonstration of their capacity to raise their groups to unmatched levels.

The global acknowledgment and grants gave to these legends become the outside approvals of their ability. Thinking back on the awards got, they recognize the job these distinctions played in molding their ways of life as worldwide symbols. The singular acknowledgment, whether as Ballon d'Or grants or other lofty titles, turns into a demonstration of their effect on the game's story and their persevering through impact on people in the future.

Passing the light to the cutting edge turns into a powerful subject in the impressions of these legends. As they change from dynamic playing professions to mentorship jobs, they perceive the obligation of sustaining the gifts that will convey the heritage forward. The reflections on mentorship highlight the repetitive idea of football, where the previous hopeful youth become the present directing coaches, guaranteeing the interminability of the game's practices, values, and greatness.

In the reflections on thinking back on an unbelievable vocation, the legends perceive the cooperative connection between their own excursions and the more extensive story of football's development. Their singular stories become strings woven into the rich embroidery of the game's set of experiences, adding to the continuous story that traverses ages. The lovely game, as seen through their eyes, isn't simply a progression of matches and accomplishments yet a significant and getting through social peculiarity that catches the embodiment of human soul and versatility.

9.3 The enduring impact on football culture

The persevering through effect of football legends on the way of life of the game is a diverse investigation that digs into the significant impact these famous figures have had on molding the ethos, values, and customs of football. Their heritages stretch out a long ways past the pitch, reverberating in the hearts of fans, motivating the up and coming age of players, and adding to the consistently developing story of football culture.

At the center of the getting through influence lies the unyielding soul displayed by these football legends. Their resolute obligation to greatness, strength even with difficulties, and the quest for significance act as core values that penetrate the more extensive football culture. Fans, trying players, and even individual experts focus on these legends as guides of motivation, typifying the embodiment of the wonderful game.

The effect is unmistakable in the grassroots of football, where the reverberations of these legends' accounts resound. The wannabes, binding up their boots on dusty fields and shoddy pitches, draw inspiration from the stories of the people who once remained from their point of view. The persevering through picture of an unbelievable player spilling past safeguards, scoring critical objectives, and lifting prizes turns into a wellspring of yearning for youthful gifts exploring their own excursions in the realm of football.

The social meaning of football reaches out past the actual game, becoming implanted in the social texture of networks and countries. Football legends, frequently worshipped as neighborhood and public legends, expect jobs that rise above sports. Their impact stretches out to cultural qualities, representing traits like cooperation, discipline, and persistence that reach out past the limits of the pitch. These qualities, reflected in the activities of unbelievable players, add to the more extensive social woven artwork of the areas they address.

One of the persevering through effects of football legends is the production of a common personality among fans. The faithfulness to a specific club or public group turns into a wellspring of pride and having a place. Fans unite behind the tradition of their footballing symbols, making a feeling of local area that rises above geological limits. The ceremonies of matchday, the serenades reverberating through arenas, and the aggregate festival of triumphs or sympathizing in routs all add to the dynamic football culture molded by these legends.

The persevering through influence likewise appears in the worldwide allure of football as a social peculiarity. Symbols like Pelé, Maradona, Messi, and Ronaldo rise above public boundaries, becoming worldwide diplomats for the game.

Their impact reaches out to assorted corners of the world, where fans associate with the general language of football. The game turns into a common encounter that spans social holes, encouraging a feeling of solidarity and fellowship among individuals from various foundations.

Past the quick impact on fans and networks, football legends assume a critical part in molding the expert scene of the game. Their effect is clear in the development of playing styles, strategic methodologies, and, surprisingly, the business elements of football clubs. The specialized developments presented by incredible players frequently become patterns that shape the more extensive football culture, impacting instructing ways of thinking and vital ways to deal with the game.

The persevering through influence on football culture is complicatedly attached to the stories of win and flexibility that characterize these legends' vocations. Snapshots of brightness, notorious objectives, and noteworthy triumphs become piece of the aggregate memory of football aficionados. The stories of beating difficulty, whether as wounds, losses, or individual difficulties, resound on a human level, cultivating an association between the legends and their worldwide crowd.

The persevering through influence reaches out to how football is consumed and celebrated. The ascent of advanced media has carried fans nearer to their footballing icons than at any other time. Online entertainment stages give an immediate channel to legends to draw in with their fan base, sharing experiences into their lives, preparing schedules, and off-pitch tries. This availability improves the special interaction among fans and players, adding to the democratization of football culture.

The underwriting and sponsorship scene inside football are likewise molded by the persevering through effect of legends. Their relationship with brands, humanitarian drives, and social causes add to the more extensive social impact of football past the bounds of the game. The underwriting bargains struck by unbelievable players frequently rise above the domain of sports, raising them to the situation with worldwide powerhouses with an arrive at that stretches out past customary football crowds.

The persevering through influence on football culture is additionally appeared in the customs and customs related with the game. Celebratory motions, signature objective festivals, and, surprisingly, extraordinary haircuts become notable images related with unbelievable players. These components become imbued in the shared mindset of fans, adding layers of social importance to the game.

The advancement of football design and style is one more component of the persevering through effect of unbelievable players. Their decisions on and off the contribute impact patterns football clothing, from shirts and boots to haircuts and frill.

The fashion decisions of football symbols become proclamations that reflect individual style as well as more extensive social movements inside the game.

The persevering through influence isn't exclusively bound to the on-field exploits of unbelievable players; it reaches out to their jobs as coaches and powerhouses in the improvement of future abilities. Numerous legends progress into training, the board, or ambassadorial jobs, giving their insight and encounters to the future. This mentorship viewpoint turns into a crucial part in saving the customs and values that characterize football culture.

In the domain of football being a fan, the persevering through influence is clear in the production of fan networks, ally clubs, and, surprisingly, the foundation of historical centers committed to protecting the traditions of football legends. The journey to arenas, the presentation of memorabilia, and the ceremonies related with supporting a most loved group all add to the rich embroidery of football culture that is woven by the impact of famous players.

The persevering through effect of football legends likewise stretches out to how the game is archived and celebrated through different types of media. Books, narratives, and biopics devoted to the lives and professions of these symbols become social antiques that add to the more extensive account of football history. The narrating around amazing players adds layers of profundity to their effect, guaranteeing that their commitments are revered in the aggregate memory of football lovers.

The getting through influence on football culture is additionally complemented by the altruistic undertakings of unbelievable players. Numerous football symbols utilize their leverage and assets to resolve social issues, advance inclusivity, and add to admirable missions. Their off-field commitments expand the effect of football past the domain of diversion, situating the game as a power for positive change in the public eye.